W9-BGP-179

Kari Mecca's

Whimsy Flowers & Trims

sewing embellishments with RIBBON & FABRIC

KP CRAFT
Cincinnati, Ohio

Contents

Introduction

Spending holidays at my grandmother's house always included a sewing or crafting project. So naturally, growing up surrounded by creative women, my crafting and sewing enthusiasm started at a young age.

My career started with a sewing contest in *Sew Beautiful* magazine. I submitted a vintage-look dress. The dress won first place, and soon I was regularly contributing articles to that same publication. I started my business, Kari Me Away, began publishing sewing patterns and opened my web-based store, KariMeAway.com. This business fostered many roles; I became a teacher, an author and an inventor, introducing my line of patented Whimsy Tools.

Kari Me Away serves as my creative outlet to share ideas and designs. By combining publishing and teaching, I have the pleasure of interacting and creating with many people across the country. In my travels, I am often asked how I find my inspiration. My answer is two-fold, I look for details, and I experiment, sometimes over and over again.

When looking for details, I draw ideas from everything around me, but most often I find inspiration in high fashion. My favorite sources are fashion magazines, social media, runway shows and historical books. I search for clever or unique elements. While an overall design may sometimes be unappealing, often a closer look reveals one element, perhaps a pocket, a bow or the shape of a collar, that ignites a creative spark. Because I have an affinity for ribbons, I tend to look at embellishments and discern how I can recreate them. I take the time to keep my ideas organized by creating an electronic pinning board or photo album, a habit I've found invaluable. Even if you're not computer savvy, you can compile inspiration, pinning pictures and magazine pages to an old-fashioned corkboard or storing them in a drawer, a file folder or a labeled bin. No matter what method you choose, take the time to review what you save often with a fresh set of creative eyes. I'm always surprised at what speaks to me and when.

When writing the book *Sewing with Whimsy*, I compiled my favorite ideas and sewing techniques from years of sewing. Two years later came *More Sewing with Whimsy*. Determined to include new techniques, I did a great deal of experimentation. While trying to find a shortcut for making a froufrou bow, I had my lightbulb moment. Instead of having to mark forty-five evenly spaced dots on a length of ribbon and hand-stitch the bow, I realized I could wrap the ribbon around a specially designed tool. Suddenly I could create all sorts of beautiful flowers much more quickly and easily. I crafted several new flowers and trims to embellish the designs I was featuring in the book, and the more I experimented with different ribbon styles and widths, the more I knew I'd barely skimmed the surface of what I could create with my Whimsy Sticks. This book, *Whimsy Flowers and Trims*, has grown out of those endless possibilities. My hope is that these techniques bring out your creativity and become embellishing favorites, and that this book becomes a timeless treasure in your library.

Kari

Materials & Tools

This book is a creative collection of flowers, trims and embellishments made using the Whimsy Sticks tools. Learn how to make a variety of trims, flowers and medallions with delightfully simple techniques. Combine these techniques with the many ribbons, fabrics and trims available today and the possibilities are endless.

Whimsy Sticks

Whimsy Sticks are used to make playful and precise loops that can easily transform fabric and ribbons into unique flowers and trims. Provided with this book is a sample set of Whimsy Sticks. Each stick is labeled with a different letter and width—these items indicate the stick size. Carefully remove the sticks from the back of this book or purchase full-size acrylic sticks from KariMeAway.com or a retailer near you.

Whimsy Tape

The basics of making Whimsy trims are that ribbon or fabric is wrapped around a Whimsy Stick and tape is applied to hold the wraps. The stick is then removed, and the taped trim is sewn according to the desired project.

To use the sticks, you will need ¼"- and ½"-wide (6mm and 1.3cm) Whimsy Tape or other narrow, low-tack tape.

The punch-out sticks work best when the edges are smooth and straight. I recommend using fine sandpaper or an emery board to smooth the edges of the punch-out sticks, then fold a length of clear tape over the straight edges of each stick. This will make it easy to slide your ribbon off the stick.

Whimsy Sticks

Fabrics & Ribbons

Flowers and trims using various types of ribbon.

The fabrics and ribbons shown in this book showcase a wide range of beautiful colors, textures and styles. As trims and seasons change, not all materials and colors are available at all times, so keep your eyes open to new possibilities.

Each embellishment is labeled with the materials and tools used in the sample as well as suggestions for other materials that may work well. Use this information as a starting point to guide your creativity.

When selecting materials, look for styles that are appealing on both sides. A large number of embellishments feature both sides of the material.

The following is a list of the materials used in this book and their specific attributes.

TYPES OF MATERIALS

Two-sided ribbons: These ribbons are finished on both sides, such as grosgrain ribbon.

Two-color ribbons: Not only are these ribbons finished on both sides, but each side of the ribbon is also a different color or design.

Wired ribbons: These ribbons have a lightweight wire woven into the edges. Look for narrow styles for the most versatility.

Metallic ribbons or fabrics: Choose a subtly colored metallic weave, or go bold with a bright metallic weave. Look for metallic ribbons that also have wired edges.

Sheer ribbons or fabrics: Try organdy or organza in solids and stripes and made from natural or synthetic fibers.

Taffeta ribbons or fabrics: Look for solid, two-tone weaves and iridescent weaves.

Bias-cut ribbon or fabric: Choose silks, satins or cottons cut into strips on the bias. Overdyed silks and satins are especially pretty.

Linen or burlap ribbon or fabric: These materials are a heavier weave and can add texture to trims and flowers.

DESIGNS AND STYLES

Solids: Keep your color palette in mind and choose colors that coordinate or add a pop of color with a contrasting element.

Ombré: Choose trims that are shades of the same color or trims that have shading in the weave of a single trim or fabric.

Stripes, checks and plaids: If possible, choose woven materials, as woven materials in these patterns are often two-sided trims.

Geometric and dotted: Repeating patterns in trims often create intriguing patterns in the finished embellishments.

Fancy edge: Look for trims with a narrow edge, such as picot trim or mini pompoms no more than ⅛" (3mm) wide.

Textured: Add dimension with velvets, corduroy, lace and eyelet ribbons and fabrics.

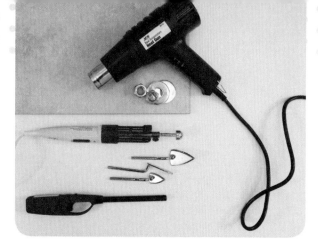

From top to bottom: Ceramic tile, heat gun, nuts and washers, mini iron with interchangeable heads, lighter stick

Tools

Having the right tools and notions can make your sewing not only faster, but easier. The items shown are featured in this book and work well for me, but they are by no means the only items available to do the job. Use the products and methods that work best for you.

Heat gun: Like a hairdryer, this gun blows heated air to curl materials. Follow the manufacturer's instructions and use caution when handling.

Ceramic tile and nuts or washers: When used with a heat gun, tile protects surfaces from the extreme heat while the nuts and washers act as weights to hold the trim.

Mini iron with interchangeable heads: Use this iron to curve loops into rounded petals and to press narrow trims. The iron can get very hot, so heat to medium and press a sample before heating any higher.

Hot/cool glue gun: This tool extrudes glue that hardens as it cools. Choose from hot and cool heating styles.

Lighter stick or candle: A flame is a useful tool for searing the ends of trim and for curling materials.

Pinning or corkboard: A pinning surface is like having another set of hands and is essential when twisting trims.

Notions

Threads: For machine sewing, choose basic sewing threads to match trims and invisible (or clear) thread when sewing on multicolor trims. For hand sewing, choose a waxed beading thread in basic colors or basic sewing threads. To add strength to basic thread, drag it across a piece of beeswax before you begin sewing.

Glass head pins: The glass heads will not melt if heated. Because sharp pins work best, indulge in new pins whenever possible.

Hand sewing needles: A milliners needle, which is a long needle with a slender eye, can be very useful when working on embellishments. When hand sewing or gathering, use a milliners size 5 or 7. If sewing beads, use a milliners size 8 or 9. If gathering long lengths of trim, a doll or upholstery needle is helpful.

Marking pens: A large variety of fabric pens is available including water-soluble, air-erasable and chalk pens or pencils. Use the method you can see most clearly on the material.

Scissors: Use sharp scissors for cutting fabrics and ribbons. Use paper or utility scissors when cutting wired ribbon because the wire will dull the blade. A small pair of pointed scissors is great for handwork. Pinking or scallop scissors are useful and also come in rotary blades for use in handheld cutters with a rolling blade.

From left to right: Fray stop glue, fabric glue, fusible tape

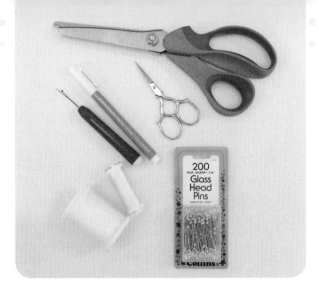

From top to bottom: Pinking shears, embroidery scissors, marking pen, seam ripper, beading and invisible thread, pins

From left to right: Starch, temporary spray adhesive, liquid basting glue, wash-away basting tape

Seam ripper: This tool is handy when cutting threads or removing stitches. The blade dulls over time, so replace it when needed.

Starch: Look for a heavy starch in a spray or pump bottle to use when shaping petals.

Stiffener: This is used to stiffen materials more permanently than starch. Use this before making raw edge fabric flowers. See the recipe on page 33.

Spray adhesive: Use a temporary adhesive spray to hold trims in place while arranging and sewing. The adhesive dissolves with exposure to air.

Liquid basting glue: Use this glue to hold trims in place instead of pinning. Because it is water soluble, it can be easily removed.

Wash-away basting tape: This double-sided tape holds trim in place, eliminating the need to pin, which is useful when applying straight trims. It is water soluble and can be removed easily.

Fray stop glue: This glue prevents edges from unraveling. It's permanent and washable, but it can sometimes be seen when dry. Test it on a sample of ribbon before using.

Fabric glue: This thick liquid glue is permanent, fast drying and washable.

Fusible tape: Look for narrow varieties of this tape that are tacky on both sides.

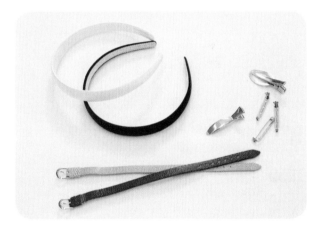

From left to right: Headbands, hair clips, pin backs

Headbands and combs: These come in a variety of colors, types and sizes. Choose a style that is comfortable.

Hair and shoe clips: These, too, come in a variety of types and sizes. When choosing a hair clip, consider the type and texture of hair.

Bracelets and belts: Consider who will be wearing these items and choose one made of a suitable material.

Pin backs and pin backs with clips: Look for items that will support the weight and size of the embellishment you have in mind. For versatility, look for a combination back that has both a pin and a clip.

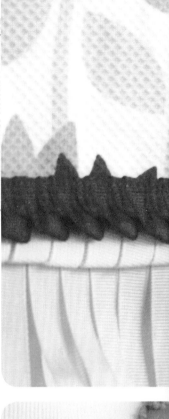

Whimsy Trims & Techniques

The very essence of these never-to-be-forgotten flowers, trims and medallions is firmly rooted in the making of Whimsy Stick trims. Become proficient at these techniques and a world of simply beautiful and delightfully clever embellishments will be at your fingertips.

The first three chapters illustrate how to make the basic Whimsy Stick trims and how adding simple alterations to those trims create an ever expanding cache of trim styles and options. The following two chapters focus on how to easily measure and mark trims, how to finish ribbon ends and attach the embellishments, and how to add accents to flowers and trims.

Each of these techniques has been carefully described, and in most cases, I have included step-by-step photos to aid in your trim-making success. Please read all of the instructions for the chosen technique before you begin.

Basic Whimsy Stick Trims

These basic techniques are the foundation for creating the captivating trims and flowers in this book. Each technique starts by wrapping ribbon or fabric on a stick and applying tape to the wraps. The stick is then removed, and the taped trim is sewn with a straight stitch. The variation in each basic technique is where the tape is applied and where the seam is sewn.

Single-Loop Trim

This trim is sewn along one edge of the wraps to create a single row of perfectly spaced loops. This is the most versatile and easiest trim to make.

 TIPS to ensure success

- If you are right-handed, hold the stick in your right hand when wrapping. Hold it in your left hand if you are left-handed.

- To quickly wrap a stick, hold the trim out taut and twist the stick, guiding the ribbon as it wraps.

- Wrap the trim, leaving ⅛" (3mm) between wraps on narrow trims and up to ¼" (6mm) on wider trims.

- Adjust wraps to be side by side, not overlapping.

- If it is difficult to remove the stick, check that the tape is not on the stick or that the wraps are not too tight.

- If wraps are too loose, twist the trim while it is still on the stick, working the fullness to the end of the trim.

- When applying tape, place the wrapped stick on a flat surface and use both hands to apply the tape.

- If needed, change the needle position or machine foot to make sewing easier.

- Shorten the stitch length when sewing narrow ribbon trims.

- If the trim is not feeding as you sew, check to make sure the tape is not stuck to the bottom of the foot or to the throat plate.

- Tape can be reused several times.

1 With the ribbon right-side up, tape the end of the ribbon to the end of the Whimsy Stick labeled "start here."

2 Twist the stick to wrap the ribbon around the length of the stick, leaving ⅛" (3mm) of space between the wraps.

3 Push the wraps toward the "start here" end, adjusting the ribbon so it lies side by side and the wraps are smooth. Continue wrapping and smoothing until the entire length of the stick is covered. If the wraps are too tight, they are difficult to remove from the stick.

4 Apply tape over the center of the wraps on both sides of the stick; this will require 2 pieces of tape.

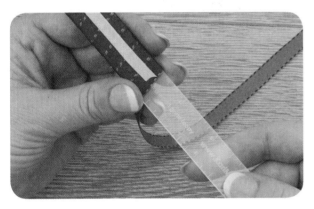

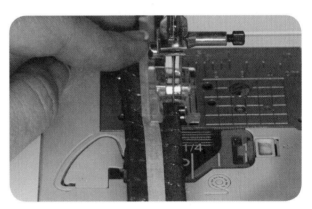

5 Remove the tape from the "start here" end of the ribbon and slide the wraps off the end of the stick. To make long lengths of trim, see the tip below.

6 After removing the stick, place the taped trim under the presser foot of your sewing machine and sew close to one edge of the wraps. Make sure you do not sew through the tape.

7 Remove the tape from the finished loops.

🌸 **TIP**

If making long lengths of trim, slide off most of the wraps, leaving 3–4 taped wraps on the stick. Repeat wrapping and taping. Overlap the tape ends when applying. Remove the stick from the wraps before sewing.

Center-Seamed Trim

This trim is sewn down the center of the wraps, creating evenly sized loops on each side of the seam. For best results, after the wrapped trim is removed from the stick, fold it in half and mark the center. This technique works best when made using a stick at least 1½–2 times wider than the trim.

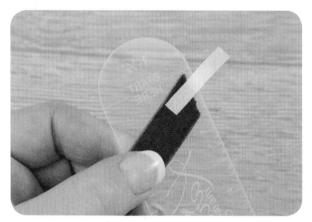

1 With the ribbon right-side up, tape the end of the ribbon to the end of the Whimsy Stick labeled "start here."

2 Twist the stick to wrap the ribbon around the length of the stick, leaving a ⅛" (3mm) space between the wraps.

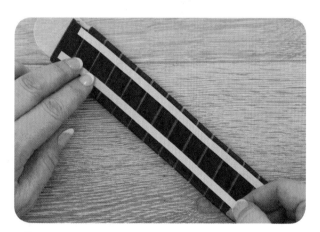

3 Push the wraps toward "start here," adjusting the ribbon so it lies side by side and the wraps are smooth. Continue wrapping and smoothing until the entire length of the stick is covered. If the wraps are too tight, they are difficult to remove from the stick. Apply tape along both edges of the wraps on both sides of the stick; this will require 4 pieces of tape.

4 Remove the tape at the "start here" end of the ribbon and slide the wraps off the end of the stick. Remove the stick from the wraps before sewing. To make long lengths of trim, see the tip with Single-Loop Trim (page 13).

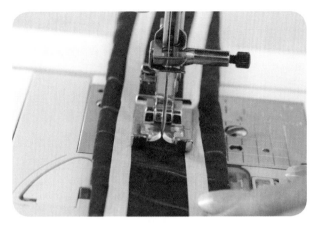

5 After removing the stick, place the taped trim under the presser foot of your sewing machine and sew down the center of the wraps, making sure you do not sew through the tape. You may want shorten the stitch length for extra strength.

6 Remove the tape from the finished loops.

Off-Center Seamed Trim

This trim is sewn off-center of the wraps, creating different sized loops on each side of the seam. The difference in the loop lengths are twice the measurement of the off-center seam. (So if the trim is sewn ¼" [6mm] from the center, the loop lengths will differ by a ½" [1.3cm]). This technique works best when made using a stick at least 1½–2 times wider than the trim.

1 Wrap and tape the trim as instructed in steps 1–4 of Center-Seamed Trim.

2 After removing the stick, place the taped trim under the presser foot of your sewing machine and sew down the wraps off-center. The degree of "off-center" is determined by the project.

3 Remove the tape from the finished loops.

Double-Loop Trim

The double loops of this trim are made by folding the wrapped trim. The two rows of loops are not only evenly spaced but also perfectly offset with very little effort. This technique works best when made using a stick at least 1½–2 times wider than the ribbon.

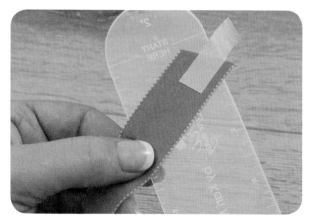

1 With the ribbon right-side up, tape the end of the ribbon to the end of the Whimsy Stick labeled "start here."

2 Twist the stick to wrap the ribbon around the length of the stick, leaving a ⅛" (3mm) space between the wraps.

3 Push the wraps toward "start here," adjusting the ribbon so it lies side by side and the wraps are -smooth. Continue wrapping and smoothing until the entire length of the stick is covered. If the wraps are too tight, they are difficult to remove from the stick. Apply tape over the edges of the wraps on both sides of the stick; this will require 4 pieces of tape.

4 Remove the tape at the "start here" end of the ribbon and slide the wraps off the end of the stick. Remove the stick from the wraps before sewing. To make long lengths of trim, see the tip with Single-Loop Trim (page 13).

5 After removing the stick, place the taped trim under the presser foot of your sewing machine and sew down the center of the wraps, making sure you do not sew through the tape.

6 Remove both pieces of tape from the top wraps. Leave the remaining 2 pieces of tape on the underside of the wraps.

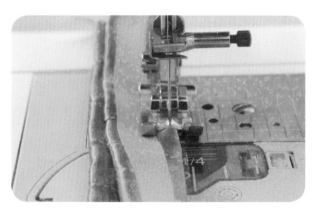

7 Fold the loops in half with the tape on the outside and offset the loops slightly. Sew close to the folded edge.

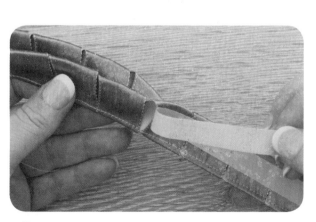

8 Remove the tape from the finished loops.

Double-loop trims add twice the number of loops with very little effort, like in these playful Double Daisies.

Beyond Basic Whimsy Stick Trims

This chapter demonstrates that by making a few simple changes to the basic techniques, new trims are possible. The modifications in these techniques are added while wrapping the stick. Take the time to read all the instructions before you begin, and follow the Basic Whimsy Stick Tips to Ensure Success (page 12).

Pointed Trims

To make points in the basic trims, the ribbon is twisted as it is wrapped. To have sharp points, make trim from wired ribbon; for soft folds, use unwired ribbons Twist the trim *up* a half turn unless stated otherwise (the result is different if you twist down).

SINGLE-LOOP POINTED TRIM

To make points in trim, the ribbon is twisted along one edge of the stick as it is wrapped. Make this trim with a two-sided ribbon. One side of a loop shows the right side of the ribbon, and the second side shows the wrong side of the ribbon.

1 With the ribbon right-side up, tape the end of the ribbon to the end of the Whimsy Stick labeled "start here." Wrap the ribbon around the length of stick, twisting the ribbon *up* on one edge of the stick. The twist is a half turn of the ribbon.

Pointed Double Daisies bloom in all sizes.

2 Continue wrapping and twisting the ribbon around the Whimsy Stick, keeping the twist on the edge of the stick if possible.

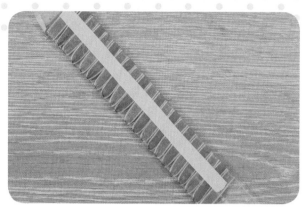

3 Apply tape over the center of the wraps on both sides of the stick.

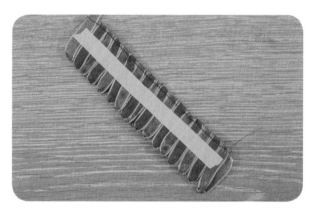

4 Remove the tape at the "start here" end of the ribbon and slide the wraps off the stick. Flatten the edges of the trim if using wired ribbon. Place the taped trim under the presser foot of your sewing machine and sew close to the untwisted edge of the wraps, making sure you do not sew through the tape.

5 Remove the tape from the finished loops. Fan the loops into a slightly rounded shape by pulling the sides.

DOUBLE-LOOP POINTED TRIM

To make points in this trim, the ribbon is twisted along both edges of the stick as it is wrapped. Make this trim using a stick at least 4–5 times wider than the ribbon. The back row of loops has the right side of the trim showing, and the front row of loops has the wrong side of the trim showing, so use a two-sided ribbon for best results.

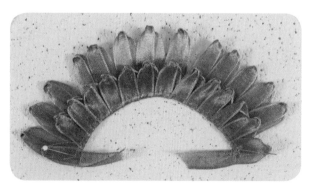

1 Make a double-loop trim (page 16), but twist the ribbon *up* on both edges of the stick. The twist is a half turn of the ribbon.

Multicolored Trims

By wrapping a stick with more than one ribbon at a time, unique trims are easy to accomplish. This technique works best when made using a stick as wide as the total width of ribbon for single-loop trim and a stick that is 2–3 times wider than the total width of ribbon when making all other trims.

1 With the ribbons side by side, secure one end of each ribbon at "start here" and wrap the ribbons simultaneously around the stick, keeping the edges from overlapping.

2 Tape and sew as instructed for the single-loop trim as shown (page 12) or other desired trim.

Two-color off-center seamed trim was used to make this Spiral Medallion.

Multi-Width Ribbons

By wrapping a stick with trims of different widths, unique trims become extraordinary. This technique works best when made using a stick as wide as the total width of ribbons for single-loop trim and a stick that is 2–3 times wider than the total width of ribbon when making all other trims.

1 Choose similar trims in different widths and wrap both trims at the same time.

2 Tape and sew as instructed for the single-loop trim as shown (page 12) or other desired trim.

Two-color, multi-width double-loop trim was used to make this Double Daisy.

Special Effects

Once the trim is made, these additional touches generate compelling finishes that add character and elegance. Variations include twisting trims, separating loops, making rings and joining ends, cutting loops and finishing edges.

Twisted Trims

By adding a twist to basic looped trims, an intriguing mixture of new embellishments is formed. When twisting, all loops can lie to one side for a pleated look, or loops can alternate sides in different combinations. Make all these variations using two-sided ribbon. Each loop needs a 180° to 360° twist of the trim, so be patient and keep twisting. Sew this trim using a small seam allowance.

1 Make a single-loop trim (page 12). Secure one end of the trim to a pinning surface.

2 Twist the length of the trim, turning until all the loops lie to one side. If the trim knots, try twisting in the opposite direction. A full 360° twist is needed for each loop.

3 Pin the trim occasionally and press the folded edge of the ribbon. Apply tape to the surface of the trim to hold the twist. If desired, sew along the seamed edge.

4 Twisted off-center seamed trim (page 15) will have a long and short loop combination. Press the folded edge of the ribbon. Apply tape to the surface of the trim to hold the twist, if desired.

Zigzag Trims

If the sewing threads are cut between loops of trim, a zigzag is created. Once separated, the trim will untwist and the loops become a perfectly spaced and angled zigzag.

SINGLE-LOOP ZIGZAG TRIM

This easy-to-make zigzag trim is a refreshing new approach to using single-loop trim. Make this trim using a two-sided ribbon. The finished zigzag trim is twice as wide as looped trim.

Add a flirty faux fur collar to a purchased sweater.

1 Make a single-loop trim (page 12) using a 1.0–1.6 stitch length and a small seam allowance. Insert the blade of a seam ripper between the loops. Carefully cut the sewing threads between every loop. If you happen to cut a ribbon edge, try searing it to repair (page 29).

2 Untwist the trim to create the zigzag pattern.

TWO-COLOR DOUBLE-LOOP ZIGZAG TRIM

Two-color double-loop trim makes an intriguing zigzag trim. Each section of the finished zigzag is made of a twisted pair of ribbons. Make this trim using 2 two-color ribbons wrapped side by side. The finished zigzag trim is twice as wide as the double-loop trim.

 TIP

If working with one color of ribbon, cut the ribbon length in half and wrap the stick with two pieces of ribbon at one time.

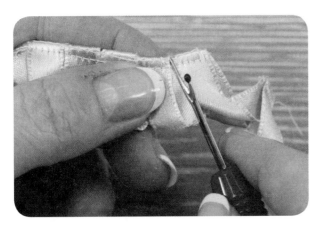

1 Make a two-color (page 20) double-loop trim (page 16). When making the trim, fold so the loops are the same length. Sew using a 1.0–1.4 stitch length. Carefully cut all the sewing threads between every loop.

2 Untwist the trim, creating a zigzag pattern that has a twist within each section.

The collar is made from rows of multicolored, multi-width trims layered in rows working from the outer edge toward the neck.

Making Rings & Joining Ends

When making many of the embellishments in this book, the first step is to form rings, or circles, of trim. When making a ring, it is important to join the trims invisibly because the seamed edge may show. Use these same techniques to join lengths of trim.

SINGLE-LOOP RINGS

Rings of trim are a basic element in many embellishments. When joining trim rings, refer to the photos to duplicate the trim ends as shown. This method features turning under the ends of the trim to finish. This is the best method of finishing if the trim's seamed edge will show.

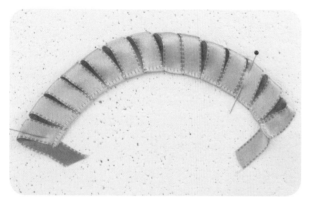

1 Make a single-loop trim (page 12). Count the desired number of loops and cut at the end of the next loop.

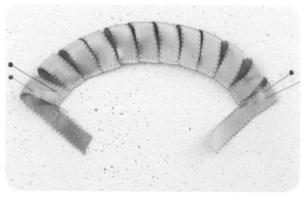

2 Fold the ribbon ends toward the seamed edge and pin. You may have to remove a few machine stitches for the ends to lie flat.

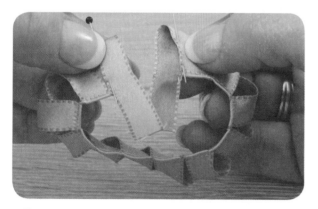

3 Form a ring by overlapping the ends and aligning the ribbon edges. Pin to hold.

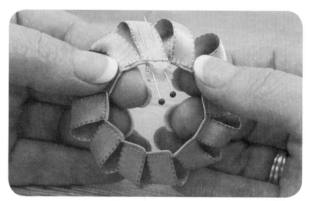

4 Sew, extending stitches beyond the overlapping ribbons as shown. Fold the ends to the back and tack in place to finish.

TWO-COLOR SINGLE-LOOP RINGS

The key to making a ring is understanding which side of the trim shows at the ends; refer to photos for each technique. This method features turning under and searing the ends of the trim to finish.

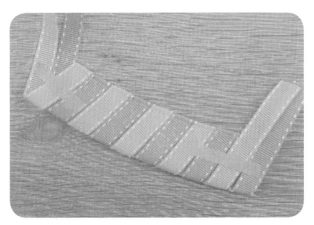

1 Make a two-color single-loop trim (page 20). Count the desired number of pairs of loops and cut at the next pair of loops. Fold the ribbon ends toward the seamed edge and tape to hold (you may have to remove a few machine stitches). Note that each end of the trim should feature opposite color loops.

Making a ring is the first step in making medallions.

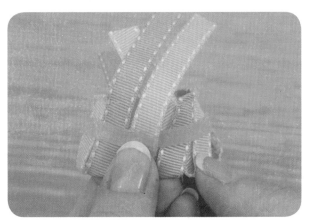

2 Form a ring by overlapping the ends and aligning the ribbon loops. Pin to hold.

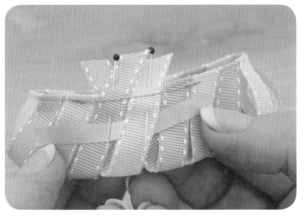

3 Sew, extending stitches beyond the overlapping ends. Turn the ends under and tack in place.

DOUBLE-LOOP RINGS

When making double-loop rings, unstitch loops as needed to match the photos. This method features turning under the ends of the trim to finish.

1 Make a double-loop trim (page 16). Counting loops, pin at the desired number of pairs. Fold the ribbon ends as shown.

2 Remove the machine stitches until the ends lie flat. Note that one end of the trim ends with the right side of the loops, and the other end of the trim ends with the wrong side of the loops.

3 Form a ring by overlapping the ends and aligning the ribbon edges. Pin to hold.

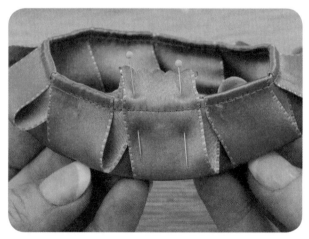

4 Sew, extending stitches beyond the overlapping ribbons. Fold the ends to the back and tack to hold.

OFF-CENTER AND CENTER-SEAMED RINGS

When making rings with center- and off-center seamed trims, it is often easier to make the ring by hand. Join the trims invisibly by using matching or invisible thread because the seamed edge may show.

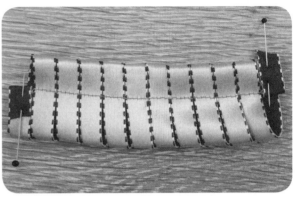

1 Make off-center (page 15) or center-seamed trim (page 14). Cut the trim at one end with the wrong side of the ribbon showing and the tail facing up. Count the desired number of loops and cut the bottom of the next loop.

2 Turn the trim over so the ribbon tails are on top of the trim (this will be the wrong side of the ring). Fold the ribbon tails along the seam and pin to hold.

3 Apply tape to hold the tails, and remove the pins. Form a ring by overlapping the ends and aligning the folded ribbon edges.

4 Hand-stitch the folds together. Trim the ribbon tails close. Sear the ends if possible (page 29).

5 Turn the ring right-side out and hand-sew along the seam where the ribbons join. Knot the thread on the wrong side to finish.

Cut-Loop Trim

By cutting the loops of a trim, the ends can be fashioned into a variety of shapes. If desired, sear, shape or curl the edges of the loops. Make this trim using a two-sided ribbon or fabric and a single-loop trim wider than the ribbon or fabric.

1 Make a single-loop trim (page 12). Cut each loop straight across the end.

2 Trim the cut ends into the desired shape, keeping the angles. A rounded cut is shown here.

3 For special effects, trim the ends with pinking or scallop shears.

Crushing

To make a vintage trim, crush to wrinkle the trim. This technique works best with metallic or wired ribbons, well-starched materials and materials made from natural fibers.

1 Loosely roll the trim onto itself. (This can be done with any type of trim.)

2 Firmly twist the trim (you don't have to be nice about it).

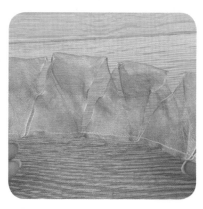

3 Unroll the trim to finish. If needed, roll and twist the trim in sections for a more pronounced effect.

Searing & Curling with a Flame

To keep edges or ends from raveling, sear or melt the ends or edges of trim or fabric using a flame. Hold the trim close to the flame longer to curl the edges. This works best on synthetic fibers because natural fibers will burn, leaving a discolored edge. Always test on a sample piece first.

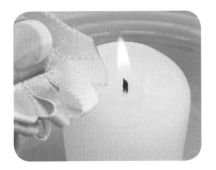

1 In a well-ventilated area, place a candle in a small dish and light the candle. Carefully hold the end of the trim close to, but not in, the flame.

2 A great alternative to a candle is a lighter stick. These are quick and easy to use when finishing ends. This method will not smoke when extinguished.

3 By holding the trim close to the flame longer, the edges will curl. Test a piece of trim to see which way the trim curls and if applying the heat to the opposite side changes the result.

Curling with a Heat Gun

You can also curl the edges of fabric and ribbons using a heat gun. Most heat guns look like a hairdryer and can be found in hardware stores. This method will not create soot on trims like a flame can. Do not use on natural fibers.

1 In a well-ventilated area, lay the trim on a nonflammable surface, such as concrete, stone or tile (I use an 18" [45.7cm] tile from a hardware store). Secure the trim with metal objects, such as large washers and nuts. Read the safety instructions that accompanied the heat gun and have a pot holder handy.

2 Test using a sample of trim. Turn the gun on the lowest temperature; pass the gun over the trim at different distances. If needed, turn the temperature up. Pass the gun over the trim until the desired effect is achieved. Remove the metal objects with a pot holder and allow the trim to cool. Reposition the trim, if needed.

This chapter will demonstrate the basic sewing techniques for working with Whimsy trims, which include ways to mark trims, methods to finish trim ends, fast and easy ways to gather trims and how to stiffen and press loops so they look like flower petals. There is also a trim-making yardage chart for easy reference.

Measuring & Marking

Yardage of Ribbon Needed for 1 Yard (91.4cm) of Trim

RIBBON WIDTH	WHIMSY STICKS™ WIDTH						# OF LOOPS PER YARD
	A (½")	B (¾")	C (1")	D (1¼")	E (1½")	F (2")	
⅛"	11 yds.	15⅜ yds.	19¾ yds.	21¾ yds.	24 yds.	26⅜ yds.	288
¼"	5½ yds.	7¾ yds.	9⅞ yds.	10⅞ yds.	12 yds.	13⅛ yds.	144
⅜"	3⅝ yds.	5⅛ yds.	6⅝ yds.	7¼ yds.	8 yds.	8¾ yds.	96
½"	2¾ yds.	3⅞ yds.	5 yds.	5½ yds.	6 yds.	6⅝ yds.	72
⅝"	2¼ yds.	3⅛ yds.	4 yds.	4⅜ yds.	4¾ yds.	5¼ yds.	57
¾"	1⅞ yds.	2⅝ yds.	3¼ yds.	3⅝ yds.	4 yds.	4⅜ yds.	48
⅞"	1⅝ yds.	2¼ yds.	2⅞ yds.	3⅛ yds.	3⅜ yds.	3¾ yds.	41
1"	1⅜ yds.	1⅞ yds.	2½ yds.	2¾ yds.	3 yds.	3¼ yds.	36
1⅛"	1¼ yds.	1¾ yds.	2¼ yds.	2⅜ yds.	2⅝ yds.	2⅞ yds.	32
1¼"	1⅛ yds.	1½ yds.	2 yds.	2⅛ yds.	2⅜ yds.	2⅝ yds.	28
1½"	⅞ yds.	1¼ yds.	1⅝ yds.	1⅞ yds.	2 yds.	2¼ yds.	24
1⅝"	⅞ yds.	1⅛ yds.	1½ yds.	1⅝ yds.	1⅞ yds.	2 yds.	22
1¾"	¾ yds.	1⅛ yds.	1⅜ yds.	1½ yds.	1¾ yds.	1⅞ yds.	20
1⅞"	¾ yds.	1 yd.	1⅜ yds.	1½ yds.	1⅝ yds.	1¾ yds.	19
2"	¾ yds.	1 yd.	1¼ yds.	1⅜ yds.	1½ yds.	1⅝ yds.	18

For metric conversions, see the Metric Conversion Cart on page 122.

ESTIMATING YARDAGE

Estimating the amount of yardage needed to make Whimsy Stick trims can be a challenge. This chart estimates the yardage needed to make 1 yard (91.4cm) of finished trim based on the Whimsy Stick size and the width of the ribbon. Keep in mind this is an estimate; one or two loops of trim can be lost every time the trim is cut. If cutting into short lengths, purchase extra yardage.

Select the Whimsy Stick size and the ribbon width, and follow the row and column until they intersect for the estimated yardage needed to make 1 yard (91.4cm) of trim.

MARKING USING WHIMSY STICKS

There are fast and easy ways to use Whimsy Sticks to mark ribbons, fabrics and trims. Use the techniques below to apply trims accurately, to evenly space flowers and trims, and to stitch at specific measurements. Mark using a water-soluble or disappearing pen whenever possible.

MARKING USING THE WIDTH OF A WHIMSY STICK

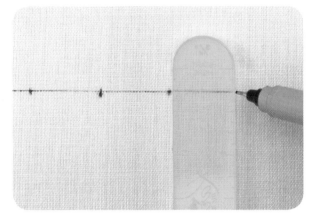

To draw perfectly spaced lines for trim placement, lay the stick of the desired width on the surface and draw lines along each edge of the stick.

To mark perfectly spaced dots for trim or flower placement, choose the stick of the desired width and mark dots on each side of the stick.

MARKING WRAPS FOR EASY SEWING

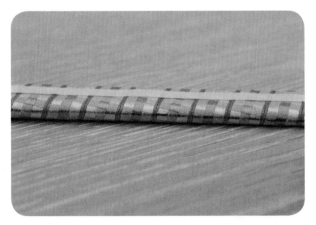

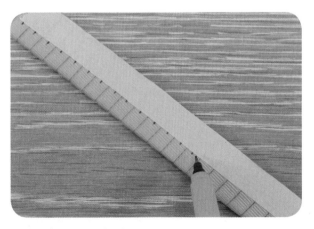

To add evenly spaced flowers or beads to a flat ribbon, wrap the trim on a Whimsy Stick and draw a line on the wraps along the edge of the stick. Unwrap the ribbon and add embellishments at the marks.

When loops need to be sewn at a certain measurement, mark dots or draw a line as a guide at the desired measurement.

Finishing Trim Ends

The best method to finish ends can vary. Review the options listed below and choose the easiest method for you that works best for the material being used.

CUTTING

Cut trim ends at an angle or use pinking or scallop shears (also available as rotary blades). There are several advantages to this method. It's quick and easy, and it's often the best method for natural fibers. If the trim ravels easily, follow with fray stop glue or sear the end (page 29).

GLUES

These are permanent glue finishes, so use products designed for fabrics whenever possible. Test a sample to determine the best choice for your project. See fray stop glue, fabric glue and fusible tape in Notions (page 9), and hot/cool glue gun in Tools (page 8).

SEARING EDGES AND ENDS

By applying heat to the ends of trims, the fibers melt together. This technique is best used on synthetic fibers because natural fibers will burn. Use a candle or a lighter (try a barbeque lighter) and hold the trim near the flame until the end melts (page 29).

Gathering Methods

There are several methods for gathering ribbons, trims and fabrics. Choose the most convenient method for the desired project. If gathering by hand, use a strong thread, such as beading thread, and sew with the thread doubled.

GATHERING AND BASTING BY HAND

The method of sewing a running stitch is a fast and efficient way to gather or baste. This stitch also enables you to take different size stitches to create different effects. This method does not work well if the threads will show or if it is difficult to hand-sew through the fabric, ribbon or trim.

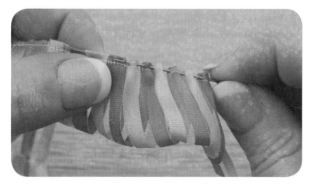

1 Thread a hand sewing needle and knot the ends together so the thread is doubled. Sew a running stitch along the edge to be gathered.

2 Pull the stitches to achieve the desired fullness and knot to finish.

GATHERING WITH SEAM ALLOWANCE

This is my favorite method of gathering because it is easy and fast. I suggest using an extra-long needle, such as an upholstery needle, to make the job easier. This method works on single- and double-loop trim only.

1 Thread a hand sewing needle and knot the ends together so the thread is doubled. Take the needle through the trim to anchor the knot. Insert the eye of the needle into the seam allowance of the trim.

2 Slide the needle through the seam allowance of each loop, pulling the needle through the trim occasionally as you work. Pull the thread to gather and knot the end to secure.

Blocking & Shaping

By stiffening and shaping trims, flat petals can be pressed into dimensional lifelike petals. Use these methods on nonwashable flowers and trims.

STARCHING AND STIFFENING

When stiffening flat ribbons or fabrics, saturate with starch or a light stiffening mixture (see the recipe below) and hang to dry. Make looped trim and, if desired, block or shape petals as follows.

stiffening mixture

In a large glass jar, mix 4 cups (1 L) of water with ¼ cup (59.1 ml) of white glue. Submerge the ribbon or fabric, put the lid on the jar and shake until the material is saturated. Squeeze the fabric or pat with paper towels to remove the excess stiffener. Hang to dry.

BLOCKING

Set the flower on an ironing board or thick towel. Hold a steam iron 2" (5.1cm) above the shaped flower and press the steam burst button to release steam. If the materials were previously starched, the burst of steam will soften the starch, which will dry once again as the shaped petal.

SHAPING

With the round head inserted, preheat the mini iron. Dampen starched or stiffened trim with water or spray-starch on nontreated trims. Place the trim on a thick foam surface and press the head of the iron firmly. For best results, push the iron down until the edges of the petals ripple. If needed, move the iron in a circular motion on larger petals (see this tool in use on page 50).

Attaching Trims & Flowers

There are countless ways to attach trims and flowers to a wide variety of surfaces. The techniques shown are featured throughout this book and are easy to use, but they are not the only possibilities. No-sew options are mentioned with the embellishments.

Sewing Techniques

The hand and machine sewing used in this book are all very basic techniques.

SEWING BY HAND

There are times when sewing by hand is not only easier, but necessary. Thread a hand sewing needle with a strong thread such as beading thread. Knot the thread ends together so the thread is doubled.

HAND SEWING A FLOWER

When tacking a flower, sew straight across the back, making sure to not distort the wraps. Sew across the flower back 4–6 times and knot securely.

SEWING BY MACHINE

When sewing by machine, the stitches are stronger and more uniform. Machine sewing is also faster than hand sewing. Thread the machine with matching or invisible thread.

STRAIGHT STITCH BY MACHINE

To attach trims using a straight stitch, sew along the trim center or along the edges with matching or invisible thread.

APPLIQUÉ STITCH BY MACHINE

To invisibly attach trims, use an appliqué stitch if possible. This stitch will have 2 or 3 straight stitches and then one stitch to the side. Align the straight stitches off the edge of the trim and the side stitches into the trim. Use matching or invisible thread.

Accents

Great accents can be anything from flower centers or leaves to a garnish sewn to trims or medallions. Look for wired vines, stamens and lace appliques. You can even cut leaf shapes from fabric or lace.

STEMS AND LEAVES

Adding greenery to a flower or an arrangement adds a natural beauty and polish. The techniques shown here include folded leaves and twisted stems. Combine these with other Whimsy Stick greenery.

FOLDED LEAVES

To make a basic leaf, cross the trim ends and sew across the base to hold.

To make a pair of leaves, fold 2 leaves, staggering the lengths, and overlap slightly. Sew across the base of leaves, stitching through all the layers.

FOLDED LEAVES ON STEMS

1 Form a leaf, leaving a tail the length of the desired stem. Take the excess trim behind the leaf.

2 Wrap the excess trim around the stem, twisting slightly. Hand-tack to hold and shape as desired.

3 Wrap several leaves together to create vines.

Beads & Buttons

Most beads and buttons make great accents, but don't overlook components in jewelry as well. Vintage pins and earrings can make stunning flower centers. The advantage in using buttons is you may need only one. Look for large or unusual buttons on vintage clothing, on the sale rack or on clothes in the back of your own closet.

BUTTONS

Look for pretty shank buttons if possible, because the sewing stitches will not show. If using buttons with holes, attach them with colored thread or add beads as you sew. Try stacking buttons in graduated sizes or group them together in a cluster. If adding buttons to a trim, sew them to trim peaks, space them across a trim or add them where trims intersect.

STACKING BEADS

Most beads can be easily sewn with the hole horizontal to a surface. When adding larger beads, the bead often looks better when the hole is vertical. By stacking beads, the small bead at the top acts as an anchor for the large bead.

1 Thread a needle with beading thread and tie a knot. Bring the needle up and thread on a large and a small bead.

2 Take the needle back down through the large bead only. Knot securely on the back of the trim.

3 Add a single stacked bead or a cluster of beads to medallions, flowers and trims.

Making a Pin

By making a flower or medallion into a pin, you can extend the wear while having limitless styling options. Pin techniques can also be used to attach flowers or medallions to headbands, shoes and purses. Shown are a few of my favorite ways to make pins.

Made with two-color satin ribbon, this flower is a variation of the Peach Peony.

If making a single flower pin, cut a piece of ribbon the width of the flower wraps (measuring from trim seam to trim seam). Apply glue to one side of the ribbon and lay it on an open pin back. Apply the ribbon to the back of the flower. This method not only adds a pin back, it can hold the flower together at the same time.

If combining several elements, cut a felt base and assemble the elements in layers, adding a ribbon and pin back to the felt base to finish.

Try adding a pop of color to a tonal dress or blouse.

Flowers, Trims & Medallions

Now that you have explored the many types of looped trims made with Whimsy Sticks, it's time to put those techniques to use. Each of the next three chapters focuses on one basic style of trim: single-loop trim, off-center and center-seamed trims and double-loop trim. The chapter Beyond Basic Trims combines all the trim styles with various other techniques and special effects. Each of these chapters includes three types of embellishments: flowers, trims and medallions.

Each of these embellishments has been carefully described with step-by-step photos to aid in your trim- and flower-making success. Each set of instructions includes notations that direct you to the basic Whimsy Stick trims to quickly refresh your memory. Use the provided skill level ratings of one (easiest) to three (challenging) when choosing techniques.

Read all the instructions for the chosen embellishment before you begin.

Single Loop

Single-loop trims are the easiest to make and the most versatile type of trim. They are also a perfect starting point to making beautiful flowers, enchanting trims and majestic medallions. Each of the embellishments begins with a basic style, and then you'll layer on new techniques and special effects to make refreshingly new flowers and trims with confidence and ease. Use the page notations to quickly refresh your memory on specific techniques when needed.

Read all the instructions for the chosen embellishment before you begin.

Single-Loop Flowers

ROSIE POSIES

This simple posie is a classic flower that looks fresh made in any color or size. Often with 4–6 petals, this flower looks lovely with beads or a button added to the center.

SKILL LEVEL: 🌼 🌼 🌼

SAMPLE MADE WITH: ½" (1.3cm) organza ribbon, A (½") Whimsy Stick and 5 loops of trim

FINISHED SIZE: 1" (2.5cm) diameter

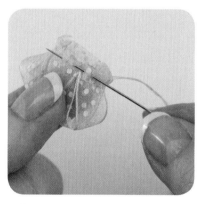

1 Make a single-loop trim (page 12) using a Whimsy Stick about the same width as the ribbon. Sew the trim into a ring (page 24) and gather along the seamed edge (page 33).

2 Pull the gathering stitches tight and knot on the back of the flower. If desired, add an accent bead or button in the center (page 36).

VELVET MUM

This mum is not only a pretty pompon type of flower, but it also works well as a flower center. It's an essential addition to fast and easy flower-making fun.

SKILL LEVEL: ✿ ✿ ✿

SAMPLE MADE WITH: ⅛" (3mm) velvet ribbon, C (1") Whimsy Stick and 34 loops of trim

FINISHED SIZE: 2¼" (5.7cm) diameter

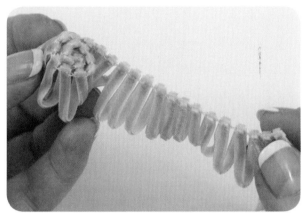

1 Make a single-loop trim (page 12) using a Whimsy Stick 3–4 times wider than the ribbon. With the ribbon ends facing the seam, wrap the trim, keeping the seamed edges even.

2 Turn the flower wrong-side up and insert pins to hold. Hand-sew or glue the back to finish.

Cheerful mums with single-loop trims are the perfect addition to this striped dress.

DAINTY DAHLIAS

These dainty dahlias combine the shimmer of metallic ribbons with the pointed petals of a wired ribbon. Make blossoms in an array of colors and sizes for enchanting possibilities.

SKILL LEVEL: ✿✿ ✿

SAMPLE MADE WITH: ¼" (6mm) metallic wired ribbon, B (¾") Whimsy Stick and 36 loops of trim

FINISHED SIZES: 2½" (6.4cm) diameter

1 Make a single-loop pointed trim (page 18) using a Whimsy Stick 3–4 times wider than the ribbon. Cut the trim to the desired length and pinch the ends of the loops to accentuate the points.

2 With the trim end facing the seam, wrap the trim loosely, keeping the seamed edge even. Turn the flower wrong-side up and insert pins to hold. Hand-tack or glue the back to finish.

3 To shape the flower, curve the first 3–4 petals into the center of the flower. Curve the next 5 petals up and the remaining petals out.

By varying the number of petals and the shade of the ribbon, you can cultivate a garden full of blooms.

Add Rosie Posies and folded leaves of metallic and organza ribbons for a beautifully finished hairpiece or pin.

WILD DAISIES

A classic flower that can be made in a wide range of colors with a varying number of petals, these sweet daisies have long, slender petals made from pointed loops with a Button Medallion center. Add accents such as a ladybug bead or mount on a stem as shown in the Daffodils (page 106).

SKILL LEVEL:

SAMPLE MADE WITH:

FLOWER PETALS: ⅜" (1cm) metallic wired ribbon, D (1¼") Whimsy Stick and 21 loops of trim

FLOWER CENTER: ⅛" (3mm) ribbon, A (½") Whimsy Stick and 12 loops of trim

FINISHED SIZE: 3" (7.6cm) diameter

1 Make a single-loop pointed trim (page 18) using a Whimsy Stick 3–4 times wider than the ribbon. Cut the trim to the desired length. Unstitch the first loop and shorten the petal by retwisting at the point.

Make daisies from a narrower ribbon for a more delicate flower.

2 Pinch to form points, or smooth to round the loop ends. Starting with the short petal and with the trim end facing down, wrap the trim loosely around your index finger 3 times. If you would prefer to count loops, have 5 loops in the first wrap, 7 loops in the second and 9 loops in the last. Keep the seamed edges even.

The red headband and bow mirror the waistline of the dress, while the flower trims complete the look.

3 Turn the flower wrong-side up and pin to hold. Baste around the wraps easing in the fullness as you work, leaving a hole in the center of flower. If needed, pull the stitches to slightly gather.

4 To finish, curve the petals outward. Add a Button Medallion (page 61) for the center.

By choosing the accent colors from the fabric, the embellishments blend beautifully without being overwhelming.

STERLING DAHLIA

This dahlia is a sterling example of how simple an embellishment can be. Made using a neutral-colored ribbon with a subtle metallic sheen, this is an easy-to-wear flower that styles into any wardrobe or home.

SKILL LEVEL: ✿ ✿ ✿

SAMPLE MADE WITH: ³⁄₈" (1cm) metallic wired ribbon, E (1½") Whimsy Stick and 58 loops of trim

FINISHED SIZE: 4½" (11.4cm) diameter

1 Make a single-loop pointed trim (page 18) using a Whimsy Stick 3–4 times wider than the ribbon. Cut the trim to the desired length. With the trim ends facing the seam, loosely wrap the trim around 6 or 7 times.

2 With the wrong side up, insert pins to hold the wraps. Hand-tack or glue the back, being careful to not pull the wraps in tight. Curve the petals out.

This elegant lily-like flower gets its roots from the Wild Daisy. Make it using soft-colored metallic ribbons and crystal beads for the center.

This is an example of how adding a pinch and a twist to the Sterling Dahlia petals can create a wildly different look.

Twisted ribbons make a great foundation for belts or bracelets. Tack with beads at each twist.

CRUSHED CARNATION

Gathering and crushing are combined to make this ruffled carnation. Pretty when made from organza or metallic ribbons, this ruffled bit of sunshine can be used as a focal flower or a fill flower.

SKILL LEVEL: ✿ ✿ ✿

SAMPLE MADE WITH: ⅝" (1.6cm) metallic ribbon, B (¾") Whimsy Stick and 30 loops of trim

FINISHED SIZE: 2" (5.1cm) diameter

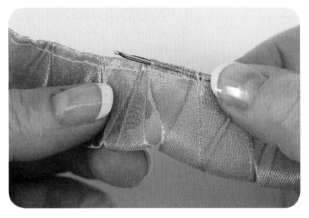

1 Make a single-loop trim (page 12) using a Whimsy Stick 1–2 times wider than the ribbon. Cut the trim to the desired length and run a gathering thread along the seamed edge (page 33).

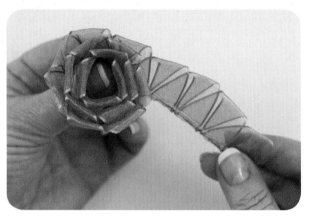

2 Loosely wrap the trim 3–4 times and pin to hold.

3 Pull the gathering thread from both the knot end and the needle end. Adjust the gathers, if needed, and knot the threads. Hand-tack to finish.

4 Crush the petals by rolling the flower firmly between your hands. Adjust the petals as needed.

BLUE CAMELLIA

A variation of the Crushed Carnation, these camellias have shaped and seared petals. By cutting the petals, both sides of the fabric are showcased, adding depth and richness to the texture and color.

SKILL LEVEL: ✿ ✿ ✿

SAMPLE MADE WITH: 1½" (3.8cm) synthetic taffeta ribbon or fabric strips, E (1½") Whimsy Stick and 15 loops of trim

FINISHED SIZE: 3½" (8.9cm) diameter

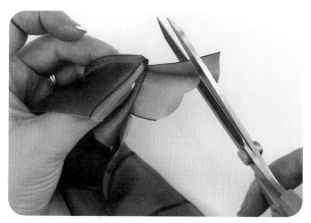

1 Make a single-loop trim (page 12) using a Whimsy Stick 1–2 times wider than the ribbon or fabric strip. Cut the trim to the desired length. Cut the loops and round the ends as shown (page 28).

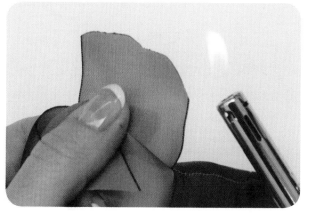

2 Sear the petal edges, curling the edges slightly (page 29). Make as instructed in the Crushed Carnation (page 48).

By choosing a brightly colored twill tape, this Camellia goes from elegant to playful.

SHABBY ORGANZA ROSE

Unbelievably pretty and just as sweet, this raw-edge rose is made from a strip of sheer silk organza torn on the straight grain. A variation of the Red, Red Rose, this flower is a perfect example of how a fabric or ribbon can change the outcome of any bloom.

SKILL LEVEL: ✿✿✿

SAMPLE MADE WITH:

ROSE: 1½" (3.8cm) torn strip of silk organza fabric, C (1") Whimsy Stick, 15 loops of trim and purchased stamen

WHITE ROSEBUDS: 1" (2.5cm) silk bias, C (1") Whimsy Stick and 4 loops of trim per bud

LEAVES: 1" (2.5cm) wired taffeta ribbon and lace leaf shapes

FELT: 2" × 3" (5.1cm × 7.6cm) piece of felt

FINISHED SIZE: 5" (12.7cm) diameter

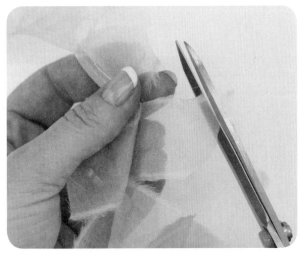

1 Tear a 1½" (3.8cm) strip of fabric. Make a single-loop trim (page 12) using a Whimsy Stick about the same width as the fabric strip. Cut the trim to the desired length. Cut the loops and round the ends (page 28). Do the same for the rosebuds using the 1" (2.5cm) silk bias.

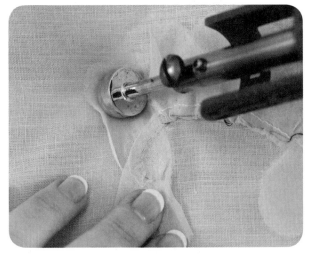

2 Starch the trim and shape each petal with the round head of a mini iron (page 8).

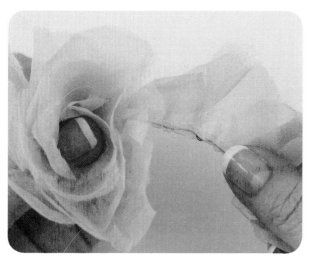

3 Run a gathering thread along the seamed edge (page 33). Gather and wrap as instructed in the Red, Red Rose (page 52), using your thumb as the flower center. Gather the buds tightly and knot to hold.

4 Insert a stamen in the flower center. Pull the gathering stitches to close the center of the flower. Hand-tack or glue the back to hold. Cut lace leaf shapes. Make folded taffeta leaves (page 35). Hand-sew or glue to a felt base, adding a pin back if desired (page 37).

Elegant in cream-colored organza, this Shabby Organza Rose is made from a cut, not torn, strip of fabric. Cut the petals in a wavy rounded shape and add a rhinestone button to the flower center. Trim with loops of taffeta ribbon.

RED, RED ROSE

Roses are timeless, and this blooming beauty is no exception. Easy to make and wear, this rose is dazzling when made in a host of colors and styles of ribbon. It's an ageless treasure worth adding to your garden of flowers. Add plaid twisted leaves to finish.

SKILL LEVEL: ✿✿✿

SAMPLE MADE WITH: 1½" (3.8cm) taffeta ribbon or strips of fabric, E (1½") Whimsy Stick, 15 loops of trim and a 10" (25.4cm) scrap of ribbon

FINISHED SIZE: 5" (12.7cm) diameter

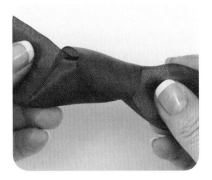

1 Tie an overhand knot in a scrap of ribbon for the flower center and pin the ends together.

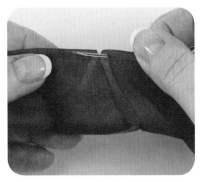

2 Make a single-loop trim (page 12) using a Whimsy Stick about the same width as the ribbon. Run a gathering thread along the seamed edge (page 33).

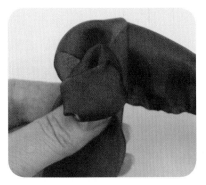

3 Lay the knotted center on one end of the trim with the raw ends facing down.

4 Pull the gathering threads slightly and wrap the trim loosely around the center, having 3 loops in the first wrap, 5 loops in the second and 7 loops in the last wrap.

5 Turn the flower wrong-side up and insert pins to hold. If needed, pull the gathering thread to ease in the fullness and knot the end. Hand-tack or glue the back to hold.

This Pointed Petals Rose is made from soft metallic ribbon and includes clustered beads in the center.

These variations of the Red, Red Rose show how changing the color or style of a ribbon, or adding beads to a center, changes the outcome of any bloom. Lay flowers on loops of taffeta ribbon and add a Flowerette bud and folded leaves.

Single-Loop Trims

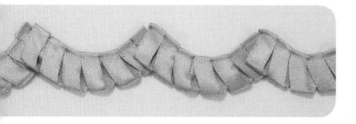

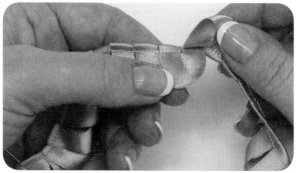

SCALLOPED SINGLE-LOOP TRIM

Scallops quickly add style and pizzazz wherever they are used. Make a scalloped trim and use it in a variety of ways: in a straight line (as shown), along in a curved line, along a seam line or extending off an edge. This trim works best when made with two-sided ribbon ⅛"–½" (3mm–1.3cm) wide.

SKILL LEVEL: ✿ ✿ ✿

SAMPLE MADE WITH: ³⁄₈" (1cm) two-color satin ribbon, B (¾") Whimsy Stick and 7 loops of trim per scallop

FINISHED SIZE: 2½" × 1½" (6.4cm × 3.8cm) per scallop

1 Make a single-loop trim (page 12) using a Whimsy Stick wider than the width of the ribbon. Count the number of loops in a scallop (7 are shown) and fold the trim up.

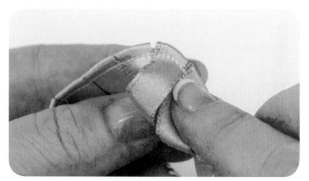

2 Pivot the trim, making the upper loop lie over the lower loop, forming a point. Pin to hold. Do the same along the length of the trim.

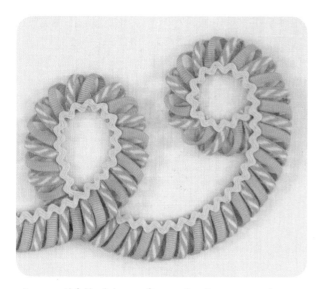

For a youthful look, loops of two-color trim are topped with rickrack.

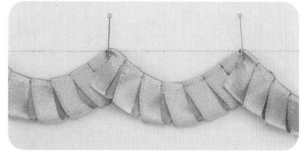

3 Draw a line and mark a dot on the fabric for each point of the scallops (shown spaced 2½" [6.4cm]). On a pinning surface, pin the scallop points to the marked dots. If sewing the trim to fabric, glue-baste in place and stitch over the trim seam.

MIRRORED SCALLOPS TRIM

With a simple twist of the trim, these scallops form an impressive border. Space twists close together for a wider, more accentuated trim (as shown), or space them farther apart for a streamlined trim. This trim is fast and easy to make.

SKILL LEVEL: ✿ ✿ ✿

SAMPLE MADE WITH:: ⅜" (1cm) picot grosgrain ribbon, B (¾") Whimsy Stick and 8 of loops of trim per scallop

FINISHED SIZE: 4" × 4" (10.2cm × 10.2cm) per repeat

1 Draw a line on the fabric and mark a dot every 2" (5.1cm). Make a single-loop trim (page 12) using a Whimsy Stick 1–2 times the width of the ribbon. Pin the end of the trim to the first dot on the line. Count the number of loops in the scallop (8 shown) and twist the trim so the loops lie on the opposite side of the trim. Pin the twist to the next dot on the line.

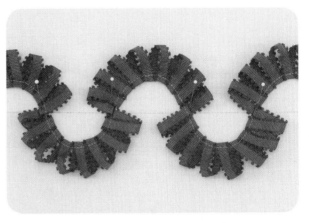

2 Do the same along the entire length of trim. Sew in place, stitching over the seam line of the trim.

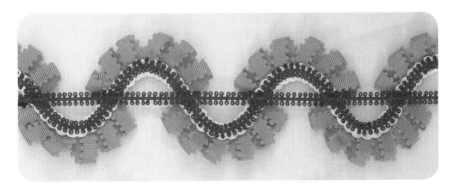

For an easy variation, add trim to the seamed edge of the loops.

TWISTED SINGLE-LOOP TRIMS

By adding a twist here and there, trims can be made to look delightfully different. Make these trims using two-sided ribbons and vary the ribbon styles and widths for different looks. If desired, add accent trim along the seam line.

SIMPLE TWISTED TRIM

SKILL LEVEL: ✿✿✿

SAMPLE MADE WITH: ³⁄₈" (1cm) two-color satin ribbon and B (¾") Whimsy Stick

FINISHED SIZE: ¾" (1.9cm) wide

Make a single-loop trim (page 12) and twist (page 21) until all the loops lie to one side.

TWISTED WAVE WITH TRIM

SKILL LEVEL: ✿✿✿

SAMPLE MADE WITH: ½" (1.3cm) organza stripe ribbon and B (¾") Whimsy Stick

CENTER TRIM: ³⁄₈" (1cm) picot grosgrain ribbon and ¹⁄₈" (3mm) striped ribbon

FINISHED SIZE: 1½" (3.8cm) wide

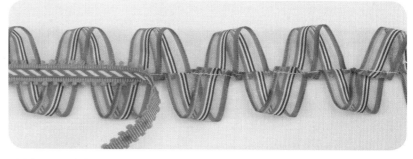

Make a single-loop trim (page 12) and twist (page 21), having one loop lie on each side of the seam. Apply an additional trim over the seam line, if desired.

TWISTED RAINBOW

SKILL LEVEL: ✿✿✿

SAMPLE MADE WITH: ¼" (6mm) grosgrain ribbon, two colors of ¹⁄₈" (3mm) striped ribbon and A (½") Whimsy Stick

FINISHED SIZE: 1" (2.5cm) wide

Make a three-color, multi-width single-loop trim (page 20). Twist the trim (page 21), making one loop of each color lie on each side of the trim.

DESIGNER ZIGZAG TRIMS

Zigzag trims are perfectly spaced and angled trims that are easy to make. Shown here made in one and two colors, these trims are best when made from a two-sided ribbon, because both sides of ribbon show equally. The finished trim is twice as wide as the looped trim. If desired, add flowers, beads or buttons at the zigzag peaks.

ONE-COLOR ZIGZAG

SKILL LEVEL: ✿ ✿ ✿

SAMPLE MADE WITH: ⅜" (1cm) picot grosgrain ribbon and C (1") Whimsy Stick

FINISHED SIZE: 2" × 2" (5.1cm × 5.1cm) per repeat

Make a single-loop zigzag trim (page 22). If needed, draw a placement line on the fabric. Let the trim untwist and align one edge of the zigzag with the drawn line. To attach, sew down the center of narrow ribbons or sew along the edges of wider ribbons.

TWO-COLOR ZIGZAG

SKILL LEVEL: ✿ ✿ ✿

SAMPLE MADE WITH: ⅛" and ¼" (3mm and 6mm) spaghetti trim and C (1") Whimsy Stick

FINISHED SIZE: 2" × 2" (5.1cm × 5.1cm) per repeat

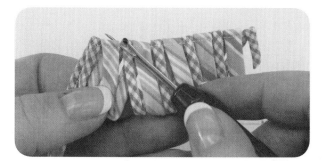

1 Make a two-color single-loop trim (page 20) using a short 1.0–1.4 stitch length. Cut the threads between each set of colors.

2 If needed, draw a placement line on the fabric. Let the trim untwist and align one edge of the zigzag trim with the line.

SCALLOPED LOOP TRIM

This trim is made by spacing the seamed edge of the loops to create open scallops. The finished scallops make 1½–2 times the amount of looped trim yardage. The wider the loops are spaced, the shorter the loops become. Make using a two-sided ribbon.

SKILL LEVEL: ✿ ✿ ✿

SAMPLE MADE WITH: ⅜" (1cm) two-color ribbon and B (¾") Whimsy Stick

FINISHED SIZE: 1" × 1" (2.5cm × 2.5cm) per repeat

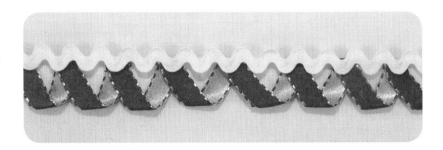

1 Make a single-loop zigzag trim (page 22). Sew the trim with a 1.5–1.8 stitch length.

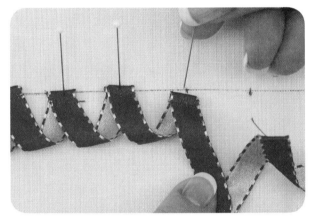

2 Draw a placement line and mark dots at an even distance for peaks (¾" [1.9cm] shown). Center the peaks at the dots and pin in place, twisting the trim as you work. If desired, add accent trim to the seamed edge or apply scallops to the edge of the fabric, allowing the loops to extend.

Layer loops of trim along a hemline.

FEATHERED FRINGE TRIMS

By cutting the loops of trim at angles, a feathery fringe is made. To layer rows of fringe, overlap each row slightly. You can also alternate colored rows of fringe for a shaded finish. For a chic look, make fringe from narrow bias-cut strips of fabric. This trim uses a large amount of ribbon. Refer to the yardage chart (page 30) before beginning.

SKILL LEVEL: ❀ ❀ ❀

SAMPLE MADE WITH: ⅜" (1cm) two-color satin ribbon and E (1½") Whimsy Stick

FINISHED SIZE: 1¾" (4.5cm) long

1 Make a single-loop trim (page 12) using a Whimsy Stick 3–6 times wider than the width of the ribbon. Cut the loops at alternating angles and lengths.

Take fringe into the world of flower making with these Spider Mums.

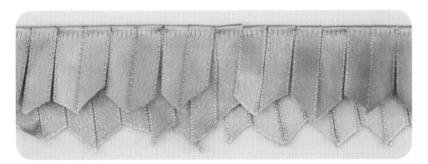

Two-color ribbons have two color options when making trims. Wrap the stick with each color facing up to see the possibilities.

Single-Loop Medallions

SIMPLE SINGLE-LOOP MEDALLION

This simple medallion is a versatile embellishment that can be used as an ornament, bud or flower center. It is also a great starting point for more intricate medallions.

SKILL LEVEL: ✿ ✿ ✿
SAMPLE MADE WITH: ⅜" (1cm) two-color satin ribbon, B (¾") Whimsy Stick and 9 loops of trim
FINISHED SIZE: 1¼" (3.2cm) diameter

1 Make a single-loop trim (page 12) using a Whimsy Stick 1½–3 times wider than the width of the ribbon. Cut the trim to the desired length and sew it into a ring (page 24).

2 Check that the loops reach the center or are longer than the center of the ring. Bring a needle up through the back edge of each loop.

3 Stitch through all the loops, sewing through the first loop a second time. Take the needle to the wrong side through the center of the ring. The stitches should lie on the inside edge of the ring.

4 With the wrong side up and using the knot end and the needle end of the thread, gather the loops into the center and securely knot.

On the right side, arrange the loops so the unstitched edges of the loops are on top of the neighboring loop. If desired, add beads or other accents to the center.

BUTTON MEDALLION

This medallion is an easy variation of the Simple Single-Loop Medallion. Because of their rounded shape, these buttons make great flower centers and buds.

SKILL LEVEL: ✿ ✿ ✿

SAMPLE MADE WITH: ³⁄₈" (1cm) two-color satin ribbon, B (¾") Whimsy Stick and 9 loops of trim

FINISHED SIZE: 1¼" (3.2cm) diameter

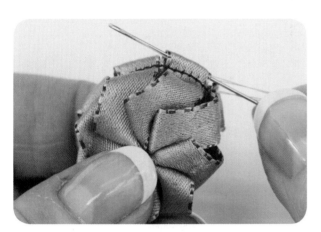

1 Make a Simple Single-Loop Medallion (page 60). Run a gathering thread along the outer edge of the medallion using the seam allowance (page 33).

2 Pull the gathering threads until the edge of the medallion turns under. Depending on the desired effect, gather, turning under the edge slightly, or pull tight for a more ball-like finish. Knot the ends securely on the wrong side.

Mix and match bright two-color trim Button Medallions with Simple Single-Loop Medallions.

FLOWERETTE BUTTON

This medallion is a variation of the Button Medallion. Because of their flowerette top and rounded shape, these buttons make superb buds as well as flower centers. This medallion looks best when made with a larger number of loops.

SKILL LEVEL: ✿ ✿ ✿

SAMPLE MADE WITH: ⅜" (1cm) two-color satin ribbon, D (1¼") Whimsy Stick and 12 loops of trim

FINISHED SIZE: 1" (2.5cm) diameter

1 Make a single-loop trim (page 12) using a Whimsy Stick 3–4 times wider than the ribbon. Cut the trim to the desired length and mark dots ½" (1.3cm) from the end of the loops using a water-soluble marker.

2 Sew the trim into a ring (page 24). Bring a needle up through both edges of a loop at the marked dots. Stitch through all the loops, sewing through the first loop a second time. Take the needle to the wrong side through the center of the ring. The stitches should lie on the inside edge of the ring.

3 Using the knot end and the needle end of the thread, draw the loops into the center so they are standing up straight.

4 Twist the loops so they lie in one direction and flatten the medallion. Securely knot on the wrong side.

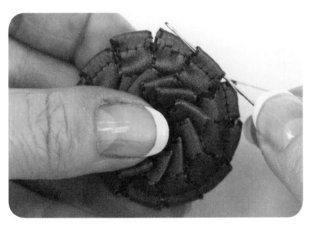

5 Gather the outer edge using the seam allowance (page 33) and pull until the edges turn under.

6 Flatten the medallion and tack, centering the gathered edge.

Layer rings of trim to create elegant blooms.

GOLDEN STAR MEDALLION

This medallion is a variation of the Simple Single-Loop Medallion. By stitching loops and tacking the outer edge, an outer ring of loops is created. This medallion looks best when made with two-color ribbons.

SKILL LEVEL: ✿✿✿

SAMPLE MADE WITH: ¼" (6mm) two-color satin ribbon, B (¾") Whimsy Stick and 9 loops of trim

FINISHED SIZE: 1¼" (3.2cm) diameter

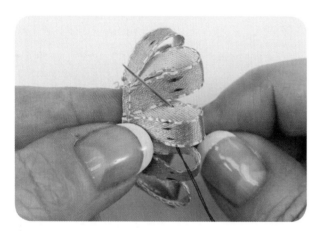

1 Make a single-loop trim (page 12) using a Whimsy Stick 3–4 times wider than the ribbon. Cut the trim to length and mark dots ¼" (6mm) from the end of the loops using a water-soluble marker. Sew the trim into a ring (page 24). Bring a needle up through the back edge of each loop at the dots. Stitch through the back of the loop only.

2 Stitch through all the loops, sewing through the first loop a second time. Take the needle to the wrong side through the center of the ring. The stitches should lie on the inside of the ring.

3 Using the knot end and the needle end of the thread, draw the loops into the center and securely knot on the wrong side. Flatten the medallion so the excess loop length extends evenly beyond the seamed edge.

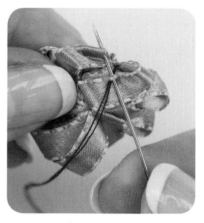

4 Bring a needle up through the seamed edge, catching the edge of one flattened loop and taking the needle down through the seamed edge of the next loop. Tack all the loops and knot the thread to secure.

SPIRAL MEDALLION

This medallion is another easy variation of the Simple Single-Loop Medallion. The spiral top is formed by folding and tacking the center loops. Make these medallions using two-color ribbons.

SKILL LEVEL: ✿ ✿ ✿

SAMPLE MADE WITH: ⅜" (1cm) two-color satin ribbon, B (¾") Whimsy Stick and 9–12 loops of trim

FINISHED SIZE: 1¾"(4.5cm) diameter

1 Make a Simple Single-Loop Medallion (page 60). Fold the loose edge of the loop back onto itself and tack at the seam line of the trim. Do the same for each loop. Knot thread to secure.

Add trims and medallions to a sundress, taking it from simple to simply sunny.

Off-Center & Center-Seamed Loops

Off-center and center-seamed trims provide amazing possibilities. By seaming down the middle of the wraps instead of along the edge, two sets of loops are created. Depending on the placement of the seam, the length of the loops on each side of the seam can vary. When twisting this trim, the loops look pleated. When twisting off-center seamed trim, the loops alternate long and short lengths. When wrapping the twisted trim, a delicate spiral is created.

Read all the instructions for the chosen embellishment before you begin.

Off-Center & Center-Seamed Flowers

TWISTED POSIE

A versatile fill flower that can be made in any color or size, this pretty posie has alternating long and short petals. Make with two-sided ribbon and fewer petals (six pairs or fewer) so the short petals will peek out.

SKILL LEVEL: ✿ ✿ ✿

SAMPLE MADE WITH: ⅝"(1.6cm) metallic ribbon, C (1") Whimsy Stick and 5 pairs of loops

FINISHED SIZE: 1¾" (4.5cm) diameter

1 Make an off-center seamed trim (page 15) using a Whimsy Stick 1½–2 times wider than the ribbon. Twist the trim (page 21) until all the loops lie to one side. Cut the trim to the desired length, making sure to have a long petal on one end and a short loop on the other. Sew into a ring (page 24).

2 Stitch a gathering thread along the inner edge of the ring. Pull the gathers and knot securely on the back of the flower. If desired, add an accent center (page 36).

TANGERINE ROSE

This quirky rose blooms in a sassy spiral of long and short petals. Perfect for ladies' wear, this rose can be unique when made in unexpected colors or prints—even an animal print!

SKILL LEVEL: ✿ ✿ ✿

SAMPLE MADE WITH: 1" (2.5cm) cotton satin ribbon, E (1½") Whimsy Stick and 15 pairs of loops

FINISHED SIZE: 3½" (8.9cm) diameter

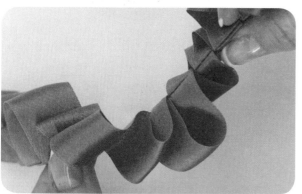

1 Make an off-center seamed trim (page 15) using a Whimsy Stick 1½–2 times wider than the ribbon. The off-center seam in the sample was sewn ¼" (6mm) from the center. Twist the trim (page 21) until all the loops lie to one side. Cut the trim to the desired length and fold the ends down.

2 Wrap the trim loosely. If counting loops, have 3 pairs of loops in the first wrap, 5 pairs in the second and 7 pairs in the last wrap. Keep the back seamed edges even.

3 With this type of trim, the petals are angled. Wrap the rose clockwise and then counterclockwise to see the difference.

4 Turn the flower wrong-side up and insert pins to hold. Hand-sew or glue the back to finish.

SWEET BRIAR ROSE

This miniature rose is a simple variation of the Tangerine Rose. By using a narrow, wired ribbon, the rose is reduced in size, and the petals will hold a soft curve.

SKILL LEVEL: ✿ ✿ ✿

SAMPLE MADE WITH: ⅜" (1cm) wired metallic ribbon, C (1") Whimsy Stick and 15 pairs of loops for the large rose or 8 pairs of loops for the smaller roses

FINISHED SIZE: Large rose is ½" (1.3cm); small rose is 1" (2.5cm) in diameter

1 Make an off-center seamed trim (page 15) using a Whimsy Stick 3–4 times wider than the ribbon. The off-center seam in the sample was sewn ⅛" (3mm) from the center. Twist the trim (page 21) until all the loops lie to one side.

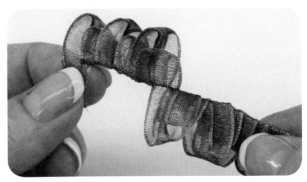

2 Cut the trim to the desired length and fold the ends down. Fan the loops by pulling the sides to round the petals. Count 3 pairs of loops and fold the trim down.

3 Holding the ribbon end, wrap 3 pairs of loops around once for the rose center. Tack the wrap at the base and curve the petals into the center.

4 Fold the remaining trim up and curve the loops out. Wrap the remaining loops loosely. Turn the wrong side up and insert pins to hold. Hand-tack or glue to finish the back.

SWEET BRIAR VINE

When assembling a floral piece, it can be eye-catching to combine at least two types of greenery. This clever vine can be folded and used as sprigs for fill or curved to build a design. Best when made from wired ribbon, this vine can also be made from other materials if you simply tack the trim to hold the twist.

SKILL LEVEL: ✿ ✿ ✿

SAMPLE MADE WITH: ⅜" (1cm) wired metallic ribbon, C (1") Whimsy Stick and 15–20 pairs of loops

FINISHED SIZE: 1¾" (4.5cm) wide

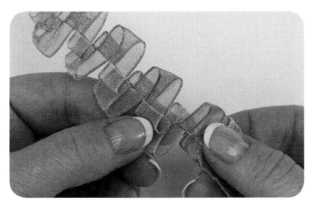

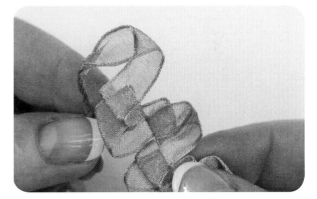

1. Make an off-center seamed trim (page 15) using a Whimsy Stick 1½–2 times wider than the ribbon. The off-center seam in the sample was sewn ⅛" (3mm) from the center. Twist the trim (page 21) until a long and a short loop lie on each side of the trim. Cut the trim to the desired length and round the loops by pulling the sides.

2. Tightly twist the ribbon end and take it to the back of the trim. Hand-tack or glue to hold. Curve the last 1–2 loops to make the pointed end of the vine. Do the same for both ends.

   Fold the trim to create sprigs of vine, or wrap it with a contrasting color as instructed in Plaid and Picot Twisted Trim (page 77).

Combine Sweet Briar Roses and Vine with Rosie Posies for an elegant embellishment.

VINTAGE ROSE

Give this rose an aged look by pressing the twisted loops flat. A slight variation of the Tangerine Rose, this rose is best when made with a two-color ribbon that will hold a crease.

SKILL LEVEL: ✿✿✿

SAMPLE MADE WITH: 1" (2.5cm) two-color satin ribbon, F (2") Whimsy Stick and 25 pairs of loops

FINISHED SIZE: 3½" (8.9cm) diameter

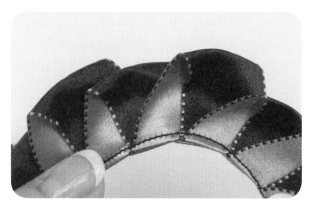

1 Make an off-center seamed trim (page 15) using a Whimsy Stick 2–3 times wider than the ribbon. Sew the trim slightly off-center and twist until all the loops lie to one side. Cut the trim to the desired length.

2 Sew the trim along the twisted edge, curving the trim as you sew. Shape the loops slightly using the round head of a mini iron (page 8).

3 Fold the trim ends down and wrap the trim. Keep the wraps loose and the back edges even.

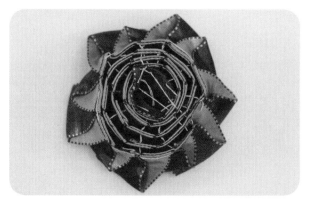

4 Turn the wrong side up and insert pins to hold. Hand-tack or glue to finish the back.

Made from torn strips of silk organza, the roses are a variation of the Vintage Rose and the ruffles are made from the excess trim. Add colored pearls to the rose centers and lace to the top of the ruffles.

Add an heirloom-style bib front and cuffs to a basic blouse to create a designer fashion piece.

TWO-COLOR MINI PEONY

When this two-color trim is twisted, the colors separate while the loops stay perfectly aligned. This gives the appearance that the flower is made from two pieces of trim. The sample shown was made with two similar colors; see the same trim made in bright contrasting colors in the Twisting Taffy Trim (page 110).

SKILL LEVEL: ✿ ✿ ✿

SAMPLE MADE WITH: ⅛" (3mm) and ⅜" (1cm) wired ribbons, C (1") Whimsy Stick and 8 pairs of loops

FINISHED SIZE: 1½" (3.8cm) diameter

1 Make a two-color (page 20) off-center seamed trim (page 15) using a Whimsy Stick 2–3 times wider than the ribbon. Sew the trim slightly off-center and twist until the ribbons lie on opposite sides. Fold all the loops to one side.

Peonies can be made in contrasting colors and with varying widths of ribbon.

2 Cut the trim to the desired length and fan the loops by pulling the sides to round the petals. Curve the petals back slightly and wrap the trim with the narrow ribbon in the center of the first wrap. Wrap with 3 pairs of loops in the first wrap and 5 in the second wrap.

3 Keep the back edges of the trim even. There will be a small hole in the center of the flower. Turn the flower wrong-side up and insert pins to hold. Hand-sew or glue the back to finish.

ROYAL COSMOS

An elegant bloom with a button center and gilded petals, this clever flower can be quickly made by twisting one piece of two-color trim. It looks best when using a narrower ribbon for the button center and when made with contrasting colors.

SKILL LEVEL: ✿ ✿ ✿

SAMPLE MADE WITH: ⅛" (3mm) and ⅜" (1cm) wired ribbons, D (1¼") Whimsy Stick and 5 pairs of loops

FINISHED SIZE: 1¾" (4.5cm) diameter

1 Make a two-color (page 20) off-center seamed trim (page 15) using a Whimsy Stick 2–3 times wider than the ribbon. Sew the trim at one-third of the width. Twist the trim until each color of loops lie on opposite sides.

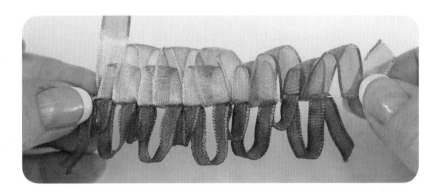

2 Fold all the loops to one side and cut the trim to the desired length. Make sure the trim is cut in even pairs. If one end starts with a long petal, the other end should finish with a small petal. Sew the trim into a ring (page 25) and gather leaving a ¼" (6mm) center hole.

3 To form the flower center, stitch through both edges of all the narrow loops of the trim. Finish as instructed in the Simple Single-Loop Medallion (page 60).

Royal Cosmos are paired with a soft white Wild Daisy for a pretty adornment.

CABBAGE ROSE

Not only does this flower work well as a rose, it can be used as a flower center, ornamental cabbage or greenery. Make using a wired ribbon.

SKILL LEVEL: ⚜ ⚜ ⚜

SAMPLE MADE WITH: ⅜" (1cm) wired ribbon, D (1¼") Whimsy Stick and 20 sets of loops for the large rose, 15 sets of loops for the medium rose or 6 sets of loops for the small rose

FINISHED SIZE: 2" (5.1cm) diameter for the large rose; 1½" (3.8cm) diameter for the medium rose; ¾" (1.9cm) diameter for the small rose

1 Make an off-center seamed trim (page 15) using a Whimsy Stick 2–3 times wider than the ribbon. Sew the trim slightly off-center and twist (page 21) until all the loops lie to one side. Cut the trim to the desired length and crush the loops (page 28).

2 Fold the trim ends down and wrap the trim.

A sunflower-like Wild Daisy with a Cabbage Rose center is combined with peach Velvet Mums, blue Button Medallion buds and folded leaves in this pretty pin.

3 Keep the wraps loose and the back edges even. Turn wrong-side up and insert pins to hold. Hand-tack or glue to finish the back. Curve the loops in slightly.

Off-Center & Center-Seamed Trims

MIRRORED GARLAND TRIM

This trim may look complicated, but it is one of the easiest and fastest trims to make. The mirrored effect is made by using both sides of a two-color ribbon. Make this trim from muted ribbon for a vintage look or bright ribbon for a fun finish. If desired, additional trim can be added over the seam line. It looks best when the off-center seam is more pronounced.

SKILL LEVEL: ✿ ✿ ✿

MUTED SAMPLE MADE WITH: ¼" (6mm) two-color ribbon and B (¾") Whimsy Stick

FINISHED SIZE: 1" (2.5cm) wide

BRIGHT SAMPLE MADE WITH: ³⁄₈" (1cm) two-color ribbon, C (1") Whimsy Stick and ¼" (6mm) spaghetti trim

FINISHED SIZE: 1¼" (3.2cm) wide

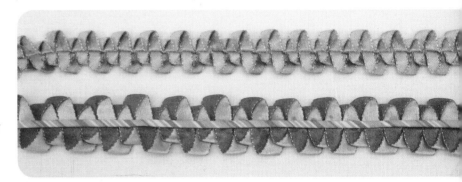

1 Cut the ribbon into 2 equal lengths, and with opposite colors facing up, tape the ends to the Whimsy Stick at "start here." Make a two-color (page 25) off-center seamed trim (page 15) using a Whimsy Stick 2–3 times wider than the ribbon. Sew the off-center seam at one-third of the width.

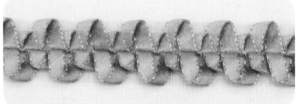

2 Twist the trim (page 21) until a set of loops lies on each side of the trim. Sew in place, stitching over the seam line of the trim.

3 Make the bright trim as instructed in steps 1–2, adding spaghetti trim to the seam line.

JUST PEACHY TWISTED SCALLOPS

This is a sweet scalloped trim made of long and short loops. Each peak is accentuated by an upward facing loop. Best when made using a two-sided ribbon, this trim can be given a new look when you thread a ribbon through the top loops as shown in Zigzag Beading (page 79).

SKILL LEVEL: ✿✿✿

SAMPLE MADE WITH: ¼" (6mm) two-sided ribbon and B (¾") Whimsy Stick

FINISHED SIZE: 2" × 1¼" (5.1cm × 3.2cm) per repeat

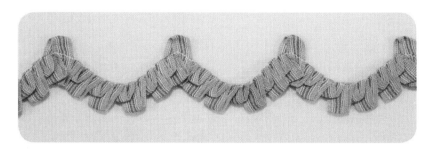

1 Draw a placement line and mark a dot for each point of the scallop (2" [5.1cm] shown). Make an off-center seamed trim (page 15) using a Whimsy Stick 2–4 times wider than the ribbon. Mark a dot on every sixth short loop. Twist the trim (page 21), leaving every marked short loop facing up. Press the trim.

2 Pivot the trim, forming a point at each up-facing loop. Pin to hold. Do the same along the length of the trim.

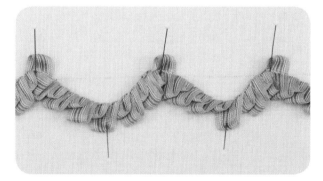

3 Pin the scallop points to the marked dots. To attach, sew the trim in place along the twisted edge.

PLAID AND PICOT TWISTED TRIM

Plaid ribbon adds a tailored look to this twisted trim wrapped with a delicate picot braid. It's pretty when used straight on the front of a blouse or enchanting when curved around the edge of a pillow. See this same trim made in solid colors and wired ribbons in the Sweet Briar Vine (page 69).

SKILL LEVEL: ✿ ✿ ✿

SAMPLE MADE WITH: ½" (1.3cm) plaid ribbon, C (1") Whimsy Stick and ¼" (6mm) picot braid

FINISHED SIZE: 1¾" (4.5cm) wide

1 Make an off-center seamed trim (page 15) using a Whimsy Stick 1–2 times wider than the ribbon. The off-center seam in this sample was sewn ⅛" (3mm) from the center. Twist the trim (page 21) until a long and a short loop lie on each side.

This softly colored version of the Red, Red Rose is combined with taffeta ribbon loops, a lace motif and beads. Staggered loops of green ribbon are added as an alternative to leaves.

2 Wrap the trim with the picot braid, placing the braid between the narrow twisted sections. Keep the tension loose.

BEADING WITH LOOPED EDGE

Beading is a trim with holes spaced to thread ribbon through. Traditionally used for gathering, this trim is also decorative. By sewing off-center, one side of this trim is beading, while the longer side is a looped edging. This is a perfect trim for the edge of a tote bag, blanket or pillow.

SKILL LEVEL: ✿ ✿ ✿

SAMPLE MADE WITH: ³⁄₈" (1cm) striped ribbon, C (1") Whimsy Stick and ³⁄₈" (1cm) ribbon for beading

FINISHED SIZE: 1" (2.5cm) wide

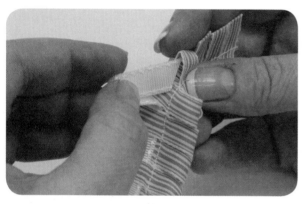

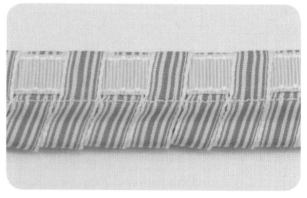

1 Make an off-center seamed trim (page 15) using a Whimsy Stick 2–3 times wider than the ribbon. Sew the off-center seam ¹⁄₈" (3mm) wider than the beading ribbon and thread the ribbon through every other loop of the trim.

2 Attach by stitching along the trim seam and the upper edge of the beading loops.

This Tape Measure Tote features single-loop beading along the top edge.

ZIGZAG BEADING

This ingenious trim combines the charm of a zigzag trim with the contrast of a beading edge. This charming band is made with two-sided ribbon and works well to join two fabrics.

SKILL LEVEL: ✿ ✿ ✿

SAMPLE MADE WITH: ⅜" (1cm) striped ribbon, C (1") Whimsy Stick and ⅜" (1cm) ribbon for beading

FINISHED SIZE: 2" (5.1cm) wide

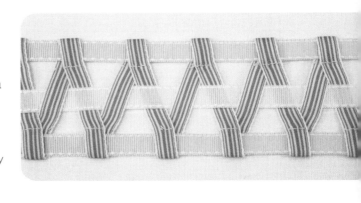

1 Make a center-seamed trim (page 14) using a Whimsy Stick 2–3 times wider than the ribbon. Sew the trim using a 1.0–1.4 stitch length. Make a zigzag trim (page 22), cutting the sewing threads between the loops on the front of the trim and in the center of the loop on the back of the trim. Carefully pull the trim to the side to separate the loops. There should be a loop of trim on each edge of the zigzag.

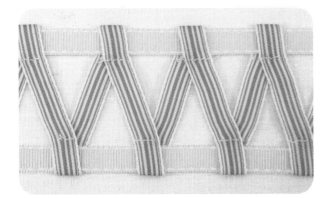

2 Thread the beading ribbon through the loops along the edges of the zigzag. If desired, weave a ribbon through the center of the trim.

Prize Medallions are charming embellishments that can be added along the edge of the zigzag beading.

Off-Center & Center-Seamed Medallions

SIMPLE LOOPED-EDGE MEDALLION

This simple medallion is a versatile embellishment that can be used as an ornament, a flower or a flower center. It is also a starting point for more intricate medallions. The seamed edge shows in the finished medallion, so join the ring carefully with matching or invisible thread.

SKILL LEVEL: ✿✿✿

SAMPLE MADE WITH: ³⁄₈" (1cm) two-color satin ribbon, C (1") Whimsy Stick and 12 loops of trim

FINISHED SIZE: 1¼" (3.2cm) diameter

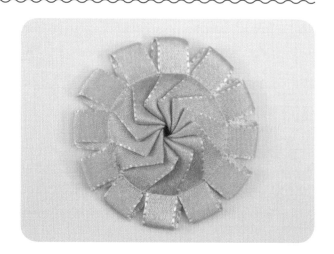

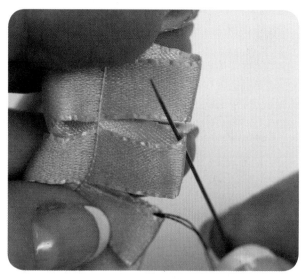

1 Make an off-center seamed trim (page 15) using a Whimsy Stick 1½–3 times wider than the width of the ribbon. Cut the trim to the desired length and make into a ring (page 27). Check that the loops reach the center or are longer than the center of the ring. Stitching through the long ends of the loops, bring the needle up through the back edge of the loop.

2 Finish as instructed in the Simple Single-Loop Medallion (page 60).

VARIATIONS OF THE LOOPED-EDGE MEDALLION

Taking the simple a step further, each of these medallions began as a Simple Looped-Edge Medallion. By folding and tacking the edges, you transform them into something delightfully new. The seamed edge shows in the finished medallion, so join the ring carefully with matching or invisible thread. Make these variations using two-sided ribbons.

SKILL LEVEL: ✿ ✿ ✿ to ✿ ✿ ✿
SAMPLE MADE WITH: ³⁄₈" (1cm) two-color ribbon, C (1") Whimsy Stick and 9–12 loops of trim
FINISHED SIZES: 1¾"–2" (4.5cm–5.1cm) diameter

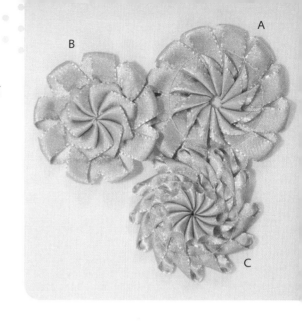

A Make a Simple Looped-Edge Medallion (page 80). Fold the loose edge of one loop onto itself and tack to the side of the loop. Tuck the fold under the neighboring loop. Do the same for each loop.

B Make a Simple Looped-Edge Medallion (page 80). Pull the loose edge of the center loop over the trim seam and tack. Do the same for all the loops.

C1 Make variation A. Have the tacked loops lie on top of the neighboring loop. Do the same for each loop.

C2 To create the pointed outer edge, fold the loops under and tack.

TWISTED STAR MEDALLION

This star is made from twisted trim with long and short petals. By tacking the short loops into the center and the long loops to the outer edge, a clever combination of points appears. This medallion looks best when made from two-sided ribbon.

SKILL LEVEL: ✿ ✿ ✿

SAMPLE MADE WITH: ⅜" (1cm) stitched grosgrain ribbon, C (1") Whimsy Stick and 10 pairs of loops

FINISHED SIZE: 2¼" (5.7cm) diameter

1 Make an off-center seamed trim (page 15) using a Whimsy Stick 3–4 times wider than the ribbon. Sew the off-center seam at one-third of the trim width. Twist the trim (page 21) until all the loops lie to one side and cut to the desired length. One end of the trim should be a long loop, and the other should be a short loop. Sew into a ring (page 24).

2 With the ring wrong-side out, sew through the end of the short loops only. The stitches will lie on the outside of the ring.

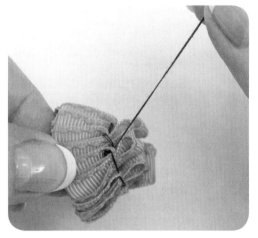

3 Stitch through all the short loops and take the needle back through the first short loop a second time.

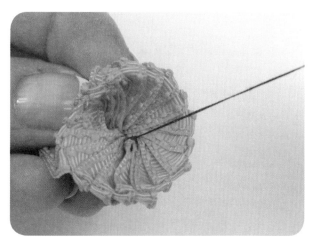

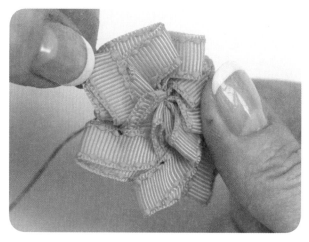

4 Turn the ring right-side out and take the needle to the wrong side. Using the knot end and needle end of the thread, pull the stitches tight and knot securely.

5 On the right side, arrange the loops so they all angle the same direction. Pull (do not fold) the long loops to the outside edge of the ring and tack to hold.

These are bright and playful variations of the Simple Looped Edge-Medallion and the Twisted Star Medallion.

These medallions feature deep-toned variations of the Simple Looped-Edge Medallion, the Button Medallion and the Spiral Medallion.

Made from various textured ribbons, these medallions are variations of the Simple Looped-Edge Medallion, the Totally Twisted and Tacked Medallions and the Button Medallion.

PINWHEEL MEDALLION

This unique medallion is made by tacking the loops so they lie across the face of the pinwheel. The secret is that the loops are very short and the trim is twisted. Make this medallion using two-sided ribbon.

SKILL LEVEL: ✿ ✿ ✿

SAMPLE MADE WITH: 1½" (3.8cm) vertical striped ribbon, E (1½") Whimsy Stick and 8 pairs of loops

FINISHED SIZE: 3½" (8.9cm) diameter

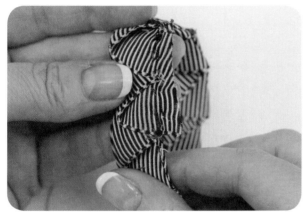

1 Make a center-seamed trim (page 14) using a Whimsy Stick about the same width as the ribbon. Twist the trim (page 21) until all the loops lie to one side. Cut the trim to size and sew into a ring (page 24).

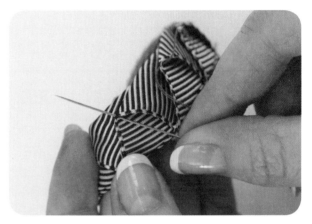

2 With the ring wrong-side out, sew through the end of each loop. The stitches will lie on the outside of the ring.

3 Stitch through all the loops and take the needle back through the first loop a second time.

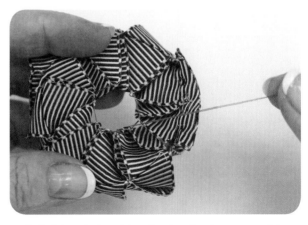

4 Pull the stitches tight, allowing the ring to turn right-side out. Knot the threads on the back. If needed, press to flatten.

Double Loop

Double-loop trim features two rows of loops for double the embellishing fun! The greatest advantage double-loop trim has is that the two rows of loops are perfectly offset and can differ in length by simply adjusting the fold. This trim also has double the number of loops, so flowers will take less finished trim.

You'll begin each of the embellishments with a basic technique and then add new techniques and special effects to make exciting new flowers and trims with confidence and ease. Use the page references to quickly refresh your memory on specific techniques when needed.

Read all the instructions for the chosen embellishment before you begin.

Double-Loop Flowers

DOUBLE PETAL POSIES

Posies are versatile blooms that can be made in any color or size. Pretty as a feature or a fill flower, these posies have a crisp look, while the metallic ribbon gives them a modern finish. The center is gathered with long basting stitches, giving the petals a pleated center.

SKILL LEVEL: ❀ ❀ ❀

SAMPLE MADE WITH: ⁵⁄₈" (1.6cm) metallic ribbon, D (1¼") Whimsy Stick and 6–8 pairs of loops

FINISHED SIZE: 2¼" (5.7cm) diameter

1 Make a double-loop trim (page 16) using a Whimsy Stick 2–3 times wider than the ribbon. Sew the trim, offsetting the loops. Cut the trim to the desired length and make into a ring (page 26). To gather, bring the needle up through the right side of a front loop. Stitch down through the left side of the loop and back up in the right side of the next loop.

2 Stitch through all the loops, making sure the threads lie over the center of each loop. Take the needle to the back and, using the knot end and the needle end of the thread, pull the stitches to gather and knot securely.

MARIGOLDS

These cheerful blooms have long and short petals to create a carefree feeling. They can be used as fill flowers or as a flower center. They are best when made with two-color ribbon.

SKILL LEVEL: 🏵 🏵 🏵

SAMPLE MADE WITH: ⅛" (3mm) two-color ribbon, C (1") Whimsy Stick and 18 pairs of loops

FINISHED SIZE: 1¼" (3.2cm) diameter

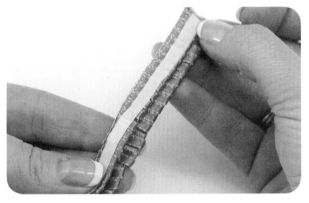

1 Make a double-loop trim (page 16) using a Whimsy Stick 6–8 times wider than the ribbon. Sew the trim, offsetting the loops one-third of the width (the first seam in the sample was sewn ⅜" [1cm] from the edge).

2 Cut the trim to the desired length. Wrap the flower with the long loops toward the center. Keep the seamed edges even.

3 Turn the flower wrong-side up and insert pins to hold. Hand-sew or glue the back to hold.

Rings of trim with button and Velvet Mum centers trim the yoke of this sweet summer sundress.

DOUBLE-LOOP ROSE

This lavish and cheerful rose is brimming with lush petals. Made from a cotton satin ribbon, this classic rose has a subtle sheen that balances the bold color of the ribbon.

SKILL LEVEL: ✿ ✿ ✿

SAMPLE MADE WITH: 1" (2.5cm) cotton satin ribbon, E (1½") Whimsy Stick, 15 pairs of loops and 6"–8" (15.2cm–20.3cm) scrap of ribbon

FINISHED SIZE: 4½" (11.4cm) diameter

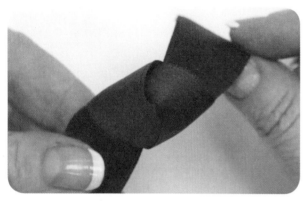

1 Tie an overhand knot in a scrap of ribbon for the flower center and pin the ends together.

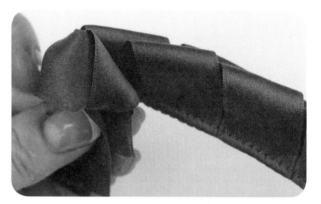

2 Make a double-loop trim (page 16) using a Whimsy Stick 1½–2 times wider than the ribbon. Sew the trim, offsetting the loops. Cut the trim to the desired length and have the ends facing the seam. With the long loops facing up, lay the knotted center on the end of the trim and align the ends.

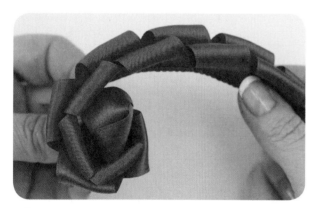

3 Wrap the trim loosely around the center, having 3 long loops in the first wrap, 5 loops in the second and 7 loops in the last wrap.

4 Turn the flower wrong-side up and insert pins to hold. Turn the flower right-side up and check the appearance. Adjust the wraps if needed. Hand-sew or glue the back to finish. If desired, add folded leaves (page 35).

DOUBLE DAISIES

These daisies are a perfect example of how rings of trim can become instant flowers. Layer ribbon rings and flower or medallion centers, mixing and matching elements for endless combinations. Although double-loop rings are shown here, any type of trim ring can be added to the mix.

SKILL LEVEL: ✿ ✿ ✿

SAMPLE MADE WITH:

FLOWER PETALS: ⅛" (3mm) striped ribbon, E (1½") Whimsy Stick and 15–20 pairs of loops

FLOWER CENTERS: Listed below

FINISHED SIZE: 2½"–3" (6.4cm–7.6cm) in diameter

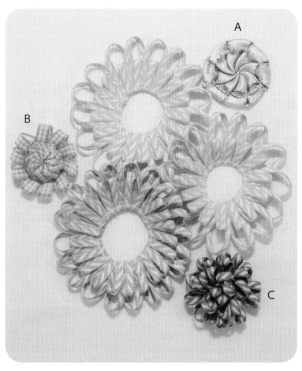

This bright Double Daisy blooms with Button Medallion buds and folded leaves.

1 Make a double-loop trim (page 16) using a Whimsy Stick 4–6 times wider than the ribbon. Sew, folding the trim at one-third the width (the sample was sewn ¾" [1.9cm] from the edge). Cut into the desired lengths and sew into rings (page 26).

2 Align a flower center in the center of a ring. Hand-sew or glue a felt piece to the back.

Choose from the following centers:
A. Spiral Medallion (page 65)
B. Simple Double-Loop Medallion (page 94)
C. Velvet Mum (page 41)

POINTED DOUBLE DAISIES

A variation of Double Daisies, these flowers have the added elegance of pointed petals. By using a two-color ribbon, each row of petals is a different color. These daisies look best when made with wired ribbon.

SKILL LEVEL: ✿✿✿

SAMPLE MADE WITH:

FLOWER PETALS: ⅜" (1cm) wired ribbon, E (1½") Whimsy Stick and 6–9 pairs of loops

FLOWER CENTERS: ¼" (6mm) two-color ribbon, A (½") Whimsy Stick and 9–24 loops

FINISHED SIZE: 3" (7.6cm) large, 2" (5.1cm) medium, 1" (2.5cm) small diameter

1 Make a double-loop pointed trim (page 19) using a Whimsy Stick 4–6 times wider than the ribbon. Sew the first seam of trim ⅛" (3mm) from the center (the sample was sewn ⅝" [1.6cm] from the edge). Sew trim into a ring (page 26).

2 Make the center as instructed in Velvet Mum (page 41). Align the flower center in the center of the pointed ring. Hand-sew or glue a piece of felt to the back to finish.

Pointed daisies bloom in an array of colors and styles.

HYACINTH

Spring is always full of surprises, and this posie is no exception. Creating dimension in a new way, this sweet bloom is made by wrapping and tacking trim to a rolled felt base. Add a fresh green flower base to finish.

SKILL LEVEL: ✿ ✿ ✿

SAMPLE MADE WITH: ⅜" (1cm) two-color satin ribbon, C (1") Whimsy Stick, 12 pairs of loops, felt rectangle 1" × 2" (2.5cm × 5.1cm) and ⅝" (1.6cm) green ribbon for flower base

FINISHED SIZE: 1½" × 2½" (3.8cm × 6.4cm)

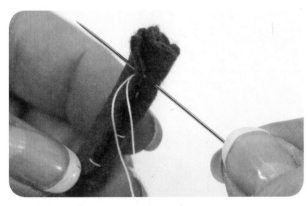

1 Roll the short side of the felt and hand-tack to hold.

3 At the base of the flower, allow the last wrap to extend slightly beyond the end of the felt (trim the felt roll if needed). Gather the bottom wrap and pull tight. Knot the thread to end. Make a flower base as instructed in Daffodils (page 106) and hand-tack to the bottom of the flower.

2 Make a double-loop trim (page 16) using a Whimsy Stick 2–4 times wider than the ribbon. Sew the trim, offsetting the loops. Cut the trim to the desired length. With the long loops next to the felt, tack the end of the trim to the top of the felt with the loops extending slightly. Wrap the trim around the felt, angling the trim down slightly as you work. Tack or glue as you wrap, loosening the wraps slightly as you work.

Make an elegant variation of the Hyacinth by using pink organza ribbon and a green metallic base and stem.

Double-Loop Trims

MULTICOLORED SCALLOPED TRIM

A playful take on a classic trim, these colorful scallops are made from a trio of bright ribbons. The double layer of loops adds depth to the trim and just the right amount of flair.

SKILL LEVEL: ✿ ✿ ✿

SAMPLE MADE WITH: Two different ⅛" (3mm) two-color satin ribbons, ⅜" (1cm) two-color satin ribbon, D (1¼") Whimsy Stick and 3 sets of loops per scallop

FINISHED SIZE: 2" × 1¼" (5.1cm × 3.2cm) per scallop

1 Make a multicolored (page 20) double-loop trim (page 16) using a Whimsy Stick 2–4 times wider than the total width of all ribbons. Count the number of loops in a scallop (the sample shows 3 sets) and fold the trim up.

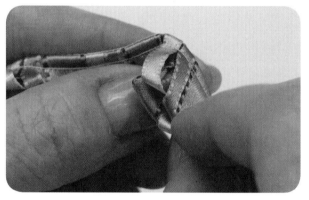

2 Pivot the trim, having the upper loops lie over the lower loops forming a point. Pin the ribbon to hold the point. Do the same along the length of the trim.

3 Draw a line on the fabric and mark a dot for each point of the scallops (the sample is spaced 2" [5.1cm] apart). Pin the scallop points to the marked dots. Sew the trim in place along the trim seam.

DOUBLE-KNOT TRIM

Evoking classic beauty and elegance, this faux knot trim is a refashioned zigzag trim. With a twist to match seamed edges, the zigzag suddenly becomes an original designer-styled trim. Shown in soft tones, it is perfect for bridal accessories and gift making.

SKILL LEVEL: ✿ ✿ ✿

SAMPLE MADE WITH: ¼" (6mm) and ⅜" (1cm) two-color satin ribbons and E (1½") Whimsy Stick

FINISHED SIZE: 1½" × ¾" (3.8cm × 1.9cm) per repeat

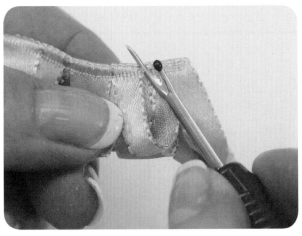

1 Using a Whimsy Stick 2–3 times wider than the total width of the ribbons, make a double-loop zigzag trim (page 23). Make the trim, folding the loops into even lengths and sewing with a 1.0–1.4 stitch length. Hint: If the remaining stitches in the zigzag come loose, pin the folds to hold before the stitches come undone.

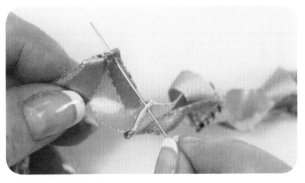

2 With the trim wrong-side up, align two folded edges and sew together, knotting securely. On the right side of the trim, there should be two loops of trim that twist.

3 Sew the next two folded edges of trim together. There will be a twisted length of trim that lies flat between the loops. To attach, hand-sew or glue in place at the back of the knots.

Double-Loop Medallions

SIMPLE DOUBLE-LOOP MEDALLION

This version of the simple medallion is a clever embellishment that can be used as an ornament, flower or flower center. Like the Simple Looped-Edge Medallion, this embellishment features looped outer edges. When the number of loops is reduced, this medallion has a star-shaped center. Add a bead center for extra sparkle.

SKILL LEVEL: ✿✿✿

SAMPLE MADE WITH: ⅝" (1.6cm) plaid ribbon, C (1") Whimsy Stick and 5 pairs of loops

FINISHED SIZE: 1" (2.5cm) diameter

1 Make a double-loop trim (page 16) using a Whimsy Stick 2–3 times wider than the width of the ribbon. Cut the trim to the desired length and make into a ring and gather slightly (page 26).

Made in a rainbow of ribbons, these medallions are perfect for babywear.

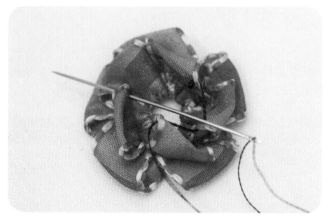

2 Sewing through the inner row of loops, bring the needle up through the back edge of each loop, sewing through the first loop a second time. Take the needle to the wrong side through the center of the ring. With the wrong side up, and using the knot end and the needle end of the thread, draw loops into the center and securely knot.

DOUBLE LATTE MEDALLION

Combining two striped ribbons in coordinating hues, this medallion would be at home as a trim in a family room or other masculine environment. Make several medallions and align on a pillow or along the edge of a lap blanket.

SKILL LEVEL: ✿ ✿ ✿

SAMPLE MADE WITH: ⅜" (1cm) and ¼" (6mm) striped ribbons, D (1¼") Whimsy Stick and 6 pairs of loops

FINISHED SIZE: 2¼" (5.7cm) diameter

1 Make a two-color (page 20) double-loop trim (page 16) using a Whimsy Stick 2–3 times wider than the total width of the ribbons. Make the trim, offsetting the loops. Cut the trim to the desired length with each end of the trim finishing in opposite colors and the ends facing the seam. Sew the trim into a ring (page 26).

2 Sewing through the inner row of loops, bring a needle up through the back edge of each loop. Sew through the first loop a second time. Take the needle to the wrong side through the center of the ring. With the wrong side up and using the knot end and the needle of the thread, draw the loops into the center and securely knot.

3 On the right side, arrange the loops so the unstitched edges of the loops are on top of the neighboring loop. Stitch through the longer loops (A) or the shorter loops (B) to make slight variations.

Beyond Basic Loops

This chapter combines all types of trims with beyond basic techniques and special effects to create unique embellishments. These richly detailed ornaments are often made in layers. Make each layer and assemble as instructed. By focusing on each step, more difficult projects can be tackled with ease.

Read all the instructions for the chosen embellishment before you begin.

Beyond Basic Loop Flowers

RED POPPY

Loops of crisp taffeta are deeply shaped into stunning flower petals. Add a feathery ring around a medallion center, and this lifelike poppy just begs to be picked. Combining several techniques, this luscious bloom can be made in a variety of colors, although it's best when made using a crisp fabric or stiffened material.

SKILL LEVEL: ✿ ✿ ✿

SAMPLE MADE WITH:

FLOWER PETALS: 2" (5.1cm) strip of taffeta, F (2") Whimsy Stick and 5 loops of trim

BUTTON CENTER: ⅜" (1cm) two-color ribbon, B (¾") Whimsy Stick and 8 loops of trim

RING: Black perle cotton, A (½") Whimsy Stick and 2" (5.1cm) of trim

FINISHED SIZE: 4" (10.2cm) diameter

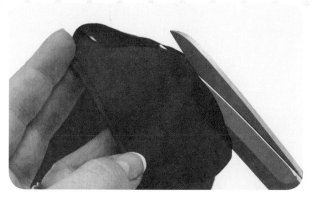

1 For the flower petals, make a single-loop trim (page 12) and cut the loops (page 28). Round the petal ends and sear the edges (page 29).

2 Spray the loops with starch until damp. Shape the petals by pressing with the round head of a mini iron on a thick foam surface (page 33).

3 Run a gathering thread in the seam allowance (page 33) of the trim. Wrap the trim twice with the petals curving in. Pin to hold.

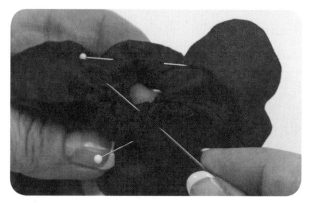

4 Pull the gathering threads and adjust as needed. Hand-tack or glue to hold.

5 For the flower center, make a Button Medallion (page 61) using 8 loops of trim.

Make a perle cotton single-loop trim (page 12). Cut a 2" (5.1cm) piece of trim and make into a ring (page 24). Cut the loop ends (page 28).

6 Layer the cut loop ring and Button Medallion into the center of the flower and hand-sew or glue in place. Fold a length of single-loop pointed trim (page 18), matching seamed edges.

OVERDYED OLD-FASHIONED SILK ROSE

This delectable overdyed silk is cleverly cut on the bias. In keeping with the name, this old-fashioned rose was hand-sewn to illustrate how easy it is to construct flowers by hand. With a Button Medallion center, it's a beautiful flower when made in any color.

SKILL LEVEL: ✿ ✿ ✿

SAMPLE MADE WITH:

ROSE: 1" (2.5cm) silk bias, C (1") Whimsy Stick and 12 loops of trim

CENTER: ⅛" (3mm) ribbon, A (½") Whimsy Stick and 9 loops of trim

LEAVES: ⅜"(1cm) wired ribbon and C (1") Whimsy Stick

FINISHED SIZE: 2½" (6.4cm) diameter

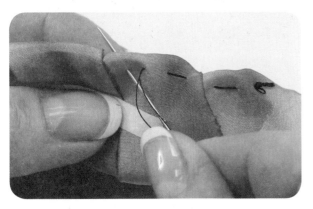

1 Make a single-loop trim (page 12) using a Whimsy Stick about the same width as the silk. Hand-baste along the edge of the loops.

2 Pull the basting threads to gather slightly. Wrap the trim around your thumb 2–3 times. Adjust the gathers if needed and hand-sew to hold.

3 Make a Button Medallion center (page 61) and insert it in the center of the rose. Hand-tack or glue to hold. Add a Sweet Briar Vine (page 69) to finish.

OVERDYED SILK PEONY

A variation of the Overdyed Old-Fashioned Silk Rose, this captivating peony has ruffled and rounded petals. Add a crystal bead center.

SKILL LEVEL: ✿ ✿ ✿

SAMPLE MADE WITH: 1" (2.5cm) silk bias, C (1") Whimsy Stick, 12 loops of trim and beads for center

LEAVES: ⅜" (1cm) wired metallic ribbon

FINISHED SIZE: 2" (5.1cm) diameter

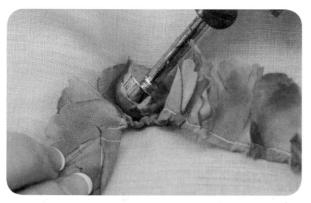

1 Make a single-loop trim (page 12) using a Whimsy Stick about the same width as the silk. Cut the loops (page 28) and round the ends using pinking or scallop shears. Spray the trim with starch and shape the petals using the round head of a mini iron on a thick foam surface (page 33).

2 Gather the seamed edge slightly and wrap the trim around 2–3 times with the petals curving in. Pin to hold and adjust the gathers so the flower center is closed.

3 Add a stacked bead (page 36) as a flower center. Make 3 folded leaves on stems (page 35) and stagger lengths.

POINTED PETALS ROSE

By making pointed trim with a soft ribbon, the petals gently fold, creating the look of a hand-rolled rose. This rose reveals the differences in twisting the ribbon and how to best arrange those twists. Finish with a curling ribbon center and leaves.

SKILL LEVEL: ✿✿✿

SAMPLE MADE WITH:

PETALS: 1½" (3.8cm) iridescent taffeta ribbon or strips of fabric, E (1½") Whimsy Stick and 21 loops of trim

FLOWER CENTER: ⅛" (3mm) two-color ribbon, C (1") Whimsy Stick and 15 pairs of loops

LEAVES: 1⅜" (3.5cm) taffeta ribbon, E (1½") Whimsy Stick and 6 loops of trim

FINISHED SIZE: 4½" (11.4cm) diameter

1 For the center, cut the ⅛" (3mm) ribbon into 2 equal lengths. With opposite colors facing up, make a two-color single-loop trim (page 20) using a Whimsy Stick 4–5 times wider than the total of the ribbon widths. Cut the loops at varying angles and sear the ends (page 29). Roll the trim and hand-sew.

2 For the petals, make 8 loops of single-loop pointed trim (page 18), twisting the ribbon *down* as you wrap the stick. Smooth the points of the trim by easing the edge of each loop into the center of the petal.

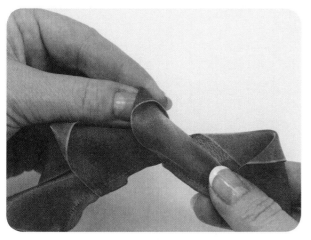

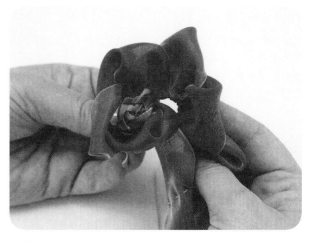

3 Make 13 loops of single-loop pointed trim (page 18), twisting the ribbon *up* as you wrap the stick. Smooth the points of the trim by rolling the edge of each loop over the top of the petal.

4 Run gathering threads in both pieces of trim using the seam allowance as a casing (page 33). Gather the 8-loop piece of trim and wrap it around the flower center 2 times and hand-sew to hold.

5 Slightly gather the 13-loop piece of trim and wrap it around the rose 2 times. Pin to hold, adjusting the petals if needed. Hand-sew on the back to hold. See the Peach Peony (page 104) for leaf instructions.

The Pointed Petals Rose is surrounded by cotton satin roses with a varying number of petals and centers. Add a Button Medallion bud and Sweet Briar Roses as accents.

SPIDER MUMS

This shaded mum makes the most of two-colored ribbons. The flower is made of single-loop rings in different combinations of ribbon color and width. Each ring has cut loops that are curled with a heat gun for a naturally styled spider mum.

SKILL LEVEL: ✿ ✿ ✿

SAMPLE MADE WITH:

OUTER RING: ⅛" (3mm) and ⅜" (1cm) two-color satin ribbons, E (1½") Whimsy Stick and 9 pairs of loops

INNER RING: ⅜" (1cm) two-color satin ribbon, B (¾") Whimsy Stick and 7 loops of trim

FLOWER CENTER: ⅛" (3mm) two-color satin ribbon, B (¾") Whimsy Stick and 7 pairs of loops

FINISHED SIZE: 2½" (6.4cm) diameter

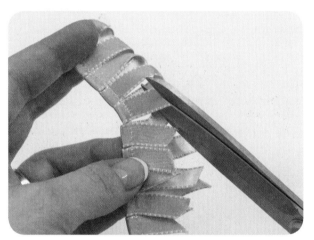

1 For the outer ring, make a multicolored, multi-width single-loop trim (page 20) using a Whimsy Stick 2–3 times wider than the total width of the ribbons. Wrap with the ⅜" (1cm) pink and the ⅛" (3mm) rose ribbons on the outside of the trim. Cut the trim to the desired length and make into a ring (page 25). Gather the seamed edge and cut the loops (page 28) at varying angles.

2 For the inner ring, make a single-loop trim (page 12) using a Whimsy Stick 2 times wider than the width of the ribbon. Wrap with the ⅜" (1cm) rose ribbon on the outside of the trim. Cut the trim to the desired length and make into a ring (page 24). Gather the seamed edge and cut the loops (page 28) at varying angles.

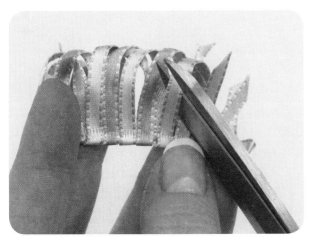

3 For the flower center, make a multicolored single-loop trim (page 20) using a Whimsy Stick 2–3 times wider than the total width of the ribbons. Cut the ⅛" (3mm) ribbon into 2 equal lengths and wrap with both colors on the outside of the trim. Cut the trim to the desired length and cut the loops (page 28) at varying angles. Roll the trim and hand-sew at the base of the flower.

4 Curl the edges of both rings and the flower center using a heat gun (page 29).

5 Center the inner ring on the outer ring and insert the flower center. Pin to hold. Hand-sew or glue the back to finish.

Make the Spider Mum from a dramatic color for a fresh look.

PEACH PEONY

Beautifully cut and softly curled, this taffeta and satin peony combines a variety of techniques and a mix of materials. Each layer of the flower is a ring, each stacked on the next with a cluster of contrasting beads for the center. For a petite variation, layer satin rings with the bead center, eliminating the taffeta petals.

SKILL LEVEL: ❀ ❀ ❀

SAMPLE MADE WITH:

TAFFETA OUTER RING: 1½" (3.8cm) iridescent taffeta ribbon or strips of fabric, E (1½") Whimsy Stick and 9 loops of trim

SATIN MIDDLE RING: ⅛" (3mm) and ⅜" (1cm) two-color satin ribbon, D (1¼") Whimsy Stick and 8 pairs of loops

SATIN INNER RING: ⅜" (1cm) two-color satin ribbon, B (¾") Whimsy Stick and 7 loops of trim

LEAVES: 1⅜" (3.5cm) taffeta ribbon, E (1½") Whimsy Stick and 6 loops

FELT BACKING: 2" × 3" (5.1cm × 7.6cm) oval

FINISHED SIZE: 5" × 6" (12.7cm × 15.2cm)

1 To make the outer ring, make a single-loop trim (page 12) and cut to the desired length. Make the trim into a ring (page 24) and gather along the seamed edge. Cut the loops (page 28) at angles with the front loops slightly shorter than the back.

Using pinking shears, cut the loops into soft points and sear the edges (page 28). Gather the ring, leaving a ⅝" (1.6cm) hole in the center. Knot to hold.

2 For the middle ring, make a multicolored single-loop trim (page 20), wrapping the stick with the lighter side of the ⅛" (3mm) ribbon and the darker side of the ⅜" (1cm) ribbon on the outside of the stick. Cut to the desired length and make into a ring (page 25). Gather along the seamed edge and knot, leaving a ½" (1.3cm) hole in the center.

Cut the loops (page 28) at angles with the front loops slightly shorter than the back. If desired, finish the loops ends with pinking shears.

Curl using a heat gun (page 29).

3 For the inner ring, make a single-loop trim (page 12) and cut to the desired length. Make the trim into a ring (page 24) and gather along the seamed edge, leaving a ¼" (6mm) hole in the center.

Cut the loops (page 28) at angles with the front loops slightly shorter than the back. If desired, finish the loop ends with pinking shears.

Curl edges with a heat gun (page 29).

4 To assemble the flower, stack the rings, aligning the centers. Hand-sew to hold on the wrong side of the flower. Hand-sew bead accents (page 36) in the flower center.

5 For the leaves, follow step 1, cutting 3-loop lengths of trim. Gather the trim to curve instead of making a ring. Hand-sew or glue in place at the ends of the felt. Center the flower on the felt and secure. If desired, add a pin back to the back of the felt (page 37).

A variation of the Peach Peony made in shades of blue with rounded, instead of pointed, taffeta petals.

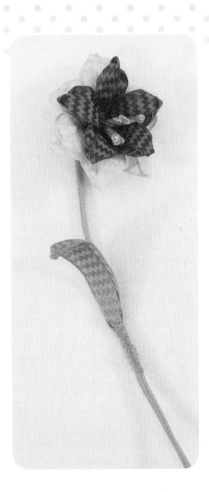

DAFFODILS

You can cultivate this springtime bloom with sunny wired ribbons. The pointed petals are easy to shape, and the tonal chevron ribbon adds color with subtle texture. With a contrasting spaghetti center, this daffodil is happily blooming atop a wired stem.

SKILL LEVEL: ✿ ✿ ✿

SAMPLE MADE WITH:

FLOWER PETALS: ⅝" (1.6cm) wired chevron ribbon in two colors, E (1½") Whimsy Stick, 5 loops of trim for upper petals and 6 loops for outer petals

STAMEN CENTER: ⅛" (3mm) spaghetti trim

FLOWER BASE AND LEAF: ⅝" (1.6cm) wired chevron ribbon, C (1") Whimsy Stick, 3 loops of trim for base and 10" (25.4cm) of ribbon for leaf

STEM: ¼" (6mm) spaghetti trim and a chenille stem

FINISHED FLOWER SIZE: 3" (7.6cm) diameter

FINISHED FLOWER ON STEM SIZE: 3" × 6" (7.6cm × 15.2cm)

1 For the flower petals, make single-loop pointed trims (page 18) using a Whimsy Stick 1–2 times wider than the ribbon. Cut the trims to the desired lengths and make them into rings (page 24).

2 With the wrong sides out, insert the upper petal ring inside the outer petal ring. Pin along the seamed edges of the rings, spacing the fullness. Sew basting stitches around the base of the flower, stitching through both rings and easing in the fullness.

3 For the stamen center, cut two 4" (10.2cm) pieces of ⅛" (3mm) spaghetti trim. Tie a knot at each end, leaving a ¼" (6mm) tail. Fold the trims in half, offsetting the ends, and tack to hold.

4 Insert the stamen in the center of the flower and pull the basting stitches to close around the stamen. Knot to hold and hand-tack the stamen securely.

5 For the flower base, make a single-loop pointed trim (page 18). Cut a 3-loop length and make into a ring (page 24).

6 Insert the chenille stem in the ¼" (6mm) spaghetti trim. Gather the flower base and insert the stem, folding the end ¾" (1.9cm). Hand-sew or glue to hold.

7 Twist the leaf ribbon 4" (10.2cm) from the end and fold at the twist. Wrap the longer end around the base of the leaf once to secure the end.

8 Lay the leaf along the stem and wrap with the remaining ribbon, turning under the end to finish. Hand-tack in place on the stem.

Hand-sew or glue the flower into the base. Trim the end of the stem if needed. Inside the end of the spaghetti trim, turn up the chenille stem ¼" (6mm). Tuck the excess spaghetti trim inside the stem to finish.

Spring daffodils bloom in pastel shades.

NIGHTSHADE FLOWERS

Deadly and delightful, these night-blooming beauties are said to be dangerous. Made from steely toned wired ribbon with bristled centers of twisted cord, these flowers have an air of menace.

SKILL LEVEL: ✿ ✿ ✿

SAMPLE MADE WITH:

FLOWER CENTER: ⅛" (3mm) silver cording, B (¾") Whimsy Stick and 2½" (6.4cm) length of trim

FLOWER PETALS: ⅜" (1cm) wired ribbon, C (1") Whimsy Stick and 12 loops of trim

FINISHED SIZE: 2½" (6.4cm) diameter

1 For the center, make a single-loop trim (page 12) using a Whimsy Stick slightly longer than the desired flower center. Roll the trim and cut at the desired size (the sample uses a 2½" [6.4cm] length of trim). Hand-sew at the base. Cut the loops (page 28) and fray the ends. Trim as needed to shape.

2 For the flower petals, make single-loop pointed trim (page 18) using a Whimsy Stick 2–3 times wider than the ribbon. Make the trim into 2 rings (page 24), having one larger than the other (the sample uses a 5-loop ring and a 7-loop ring).

3 With the wrong sides out, insert the smaller ring inside the larger ring and baste through both layers, easing in the fullness.

4 Insert the flower center and pull the basting stitches tight. Knot to hold and hand-tack the center in place.

5 Pinch the petals to accentuate the points and pull the sides to open the petal center. Curve the petals of the upper ring toward the center. Curve the petals of the lower ring out and down slightly.

When made in soft colors, the Nightshade Flower goes from menacing to magical.

Beyond Basic Loop Trims

TWISTED TAFFY TRIMS

Sweet and sassy, this trim is made using two striped ribbons in brightly contrasting colors. When twisted in various designs, the colors separate while the loops stay perfectly aligned. The same trim in softer tones was used to make the Mini Peony (page 72).

SAMPLES MADE WITH: ⅛" (3mm) and ½" (1.3cm) striped ribbons and C (1") Whimsy Stick

FINISHED SIZE: ½"–1" (1.3cm–2.5cm) wide

VARIATION 1
SKILL LEVEL: ❀ ❀ ❀

Make a two-color (page 20) off-center seamed trim (page 15) using a Whimsy Stick 2–3 times wider than the total width of the ribbons. Sew the trim ⅛" (3mm) from the center. Twist until each ribbon lies on opposite sides. Attach by sewing down the center of the trim. If desired, allow one set of loops to extend beyond an edge.

VARIATION 2
SKILL LEVEL: ❀ ❀ ❀

Twist the trim as stated in Variation 1 and then fold all the loops to one side. Attach by sewing along the folded edge.

VARIATION 3
SKILL LEVEL: ❀ ❀ ❀

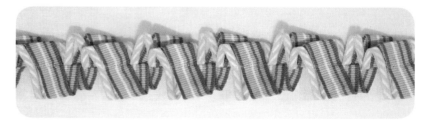

Twist the trim with a long and a short loop of each color ribbon on each side of the trim.

SCROLLING ZIGZAG TRIM

Without tedious measuring, this technique forms serpentine scrolls. This is an easy variation of zigzag trim in which every other loop is separated. The remaining loops are centered and tacked, creating the enchanting pattern in the ribbon.

SKILL LEVEL: ❀ ❀ ❀

SAMPLE MADE WITH: 1" (2.5cm) striped grosgrain ribbon and C (1") Whimsy Stick

FINISHED SIZE: 1½" (3.8cm) wide

1 Make a single-loop trim (page 12) using a Whimsy Stick about the same width as the ribbon. Separate the loops by breaking the sewing thread between every other loop. Note: There should be flat sections of trim with loops between.

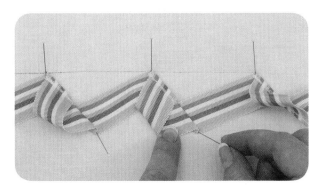

2 Draw a placement line and mark a dot every 2¾" (7cm). Pin the top edge of seams to marked dots. Smooth trim flat and pin lower seams as shown.

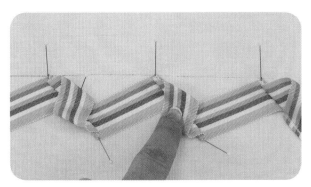

3 Flatten each loop, centering the fullness over the seam. To apply to fabric, sew the trim along the edges.

MIRRORED SHELL TRIM

Striped ribbon adds a playful touch to this artfully sophisticated trim. Made using single-loop trim, this trim becomes shells by simply adding a twist every 5–6 loops and hand-sewing as you would a medallion.

SKILL LEVEL: ✿ ✿ ✿

SAMPLE MADE WITH: ³⁄₈" (1cm) two-sided striped ribbon, B (¾") Whimsy Stick and 5 loops of trim per shell

FINISHED SIZE: 2" x 1" (5.1cm × 2.5cm) per pair of shells

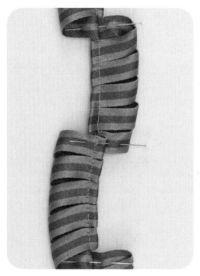

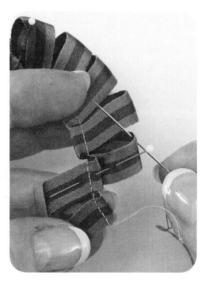

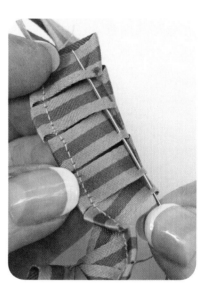

1 Make a single-loop trim (page 12) using a Whimsy Stick the same width or wider than the width of ribbon. Count the number of loops in a shell (5 loops are shown) and twist the trim so the loops lie on the opposite side of the trim. Pin to hold. Do the same along the entire length of the trim.

2 Find the twist in the trim with the seam allowance on the surface. Stitch up through the back edge of the first loop at that twist. Do the same for all loops in that shell.

3 Turn the trim wrong-side up and stitch back through the loops close to the previous stitches.

4 Using the knot end and the needle end of the thread, draw the loops together to form each shell and securely knot. Stitch all the shells on one side of the trim.

5 Turn the trim and stitch the shells on the opposite side, repeating steps 2–4. If needed, tack each twist to hold. To sew the trim to fabric, stitch over the trim seam line and hand-tack the shell peaks as needed.

This dainty shell trim would be pretty around the neck of a sweater. Make this trim using off-center seamed trim to create the outer loops and add bead accents.

ENTWINED ZIGZAG TRIM

Why choose one color when there is a rainbow? This trim makes the most of the two-color ribbon it is made from. It's another simple variation of zigzag trim in which every other set of loops is separated. The remaining loops are tacked to opposite sides.

SKILL LEVEL: ✿ ✿ ✿

SAMPLE MADE WITH: Two different ³⁄₈" (1cm) two-color satin ribbons and C (1") Whimsy Stick

FINISHED SIZE: 1½" (3.8cm) wide

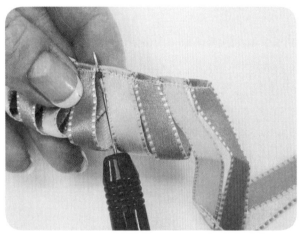

1 Make a two-color single-loop trim (page 20) using a Whimsy Stick about the same width as the total width of the ribbons. Separate the loops by breaking the sewing thread between every other set of loops. Note: There will be flat sections of trim with loops between.

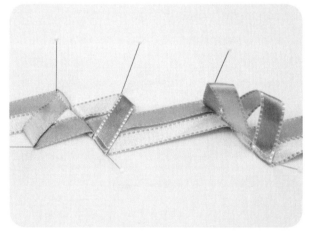

2 Draw a placement line and mark a dot every 2¾" (7cm). Pin the top edge of the seams to the marked dots. Smooth the trim flat and pin the lower seams as shown. Fold the ribbon loops on opposite sides. To apply to fabric, sew the trims along the edges.

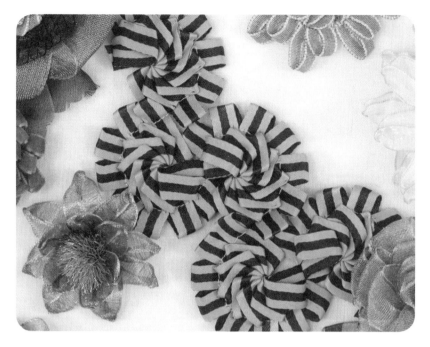

Add more loops to each shell to make the Mirrored Shell Trim wider with the shells closer together.

By tacking the loops as shown in the Spiral Medallion, this Mirrored Shell Trim showcases the two-color ribbon.

Combine trims, medallions and flowers made with different materials to create beautiful borders.

Beyond Basic Loop Medallions

TOTALLY TWISTED AND TACKED MEDALLIONS

These medallions are shown with several variations and make the most of the long and short loops of twisted trims. Made using a dainty wire-edged ribbon, the folds and twists hold their shape for easy tacking. These medallions are best when made from a narrow, two-sided wired ribbon.

SKILL LEVEL: ✿✿✿

SAMPLE MADE WITH: ⅛" (3mm) wired ribbon, C (1") Whimsy Stick and 16–18 pairs of loops

FINISHED SIZE: 3" (7.6cm) diameter

1 Make an off-center seamed trim (page 15) using a Whimsy Stick 4–8 times wider than the ribbon. Sew the trim ⅛" (3mm) off-center (the sample was sewn ⅜" [1cm] from the edge). Twist the trim (page 21) until all the loops lie to one side. Cut the trim to the desired length, making sure the trim is cut in even pairs. If one end starts with a long loop, the other end should finish with a short loop. Sew the trim into a ring (page 25).

2 Flatten the ring so all the loops lie on the outside of the ring. Stitch through the end of *every other* long loop.

3 Take the needle back through the first loop a second time. Take the needle to the wrong side through the center of the ring and knot securely.

4 With the medallion right-side up, fold the unstitched loops (sets of 3 loops) to the outside edge of the ring. Shape the outer loops, rounding slightly to finish.

VARIATION ONE
SKILL LEVEL: ✿ ✿ ✿

Make a Totally Twisted and Tacked Medallion. Fan the center loops by pulling the sides to fill the center.

VARIATION TWO
SKILL LEVEL: ✿ ✿ ✿

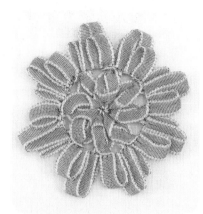

Make a Totally Twisted and Tacked Medallion. Fold the top of the center loops back onto itself and tack to hold.

VARIATION THREE
SKILL LEVEL: ✿ ✿ ✿

Make a Totally Twisted and Tacked Medallion. Locate the short loops that lie on the top of the outer loops. Fold each loop toward the center at an angle and tack to hold.

PRIZE MEDALLION

These rosettes add a celebratory touch to party favors or to certificates for sports or school milestones.

SKILL LEVEL: ✿✿✿

SAMPLE MADE WITH:

LOWER RING: ¼" (6mm) velvet ribbon, C (1") Whimsy Stick and 13 loops of trim

UPPER RING: 1" (2.5cm) striped ribbon, D (1¼") Whimsy Stick and 7 pairs of loops

CENTER: ⅛" (3mm) striped ribbon, A (½") Whimsy Stick and 55 loops of trim

FINISHED SIZE: 2½"–3½" (6.4cm–8.9cm) in diameter

1 For the lower ring, make a single-loop trim (page 12) and cut to the desired length. Make the trim into a ring (page 24) and gather along the seamed edge until the loops lie flat.

2 For the upper ring, make an off-center seamed trim (page 15) and twist (page 21) until all the loops lie to one side. Cut the trim to the desired length and make into a ring (page 24). Gather along the seamed edge until the loops lie flat.

3 For the center, make a single-loop trim (page 12) and cut to the desired length. Make a Velvet Mum (page 41) for the center. To assemble the medallion, stack the rings aligning the centers and insert the flower center. Hand-sew or glue back to finish.

Make medallions more prize-like by adding streamers. Mix and match all types of rings and centers for even more winning possibilities.

Resources

All tools and materials shown in this book can be found at the following websites:

KARI ME AWAY

www.karimeaway.com

Ribbons, fabrics, tools and materials,
as well as Kari's books and instructional DVDs.

MARTHA PULLEN

www.marthapullen.com

Tools, books, DVDs, fabrics and needles.

Index

Kari Mecca's Whimsy Flowers & Trims. Copyright © 2014 by Kari Mecca. Manufactured in China. All rights reserved. No part of this book may be reproduced in any form or by any electronic or mechanical means including information storage and retrieval systems without permission in writing from the publisher, except by a reviewer who may quote brief passages in a review. Published by KP Craft, an imprint of F+W Media, Inc., 10150 Carver Road, Ste. 200, Blue Ash, Ohio 45242. (800) 289-0963. First Edition.

Whimsy Sticks™ and Kari Me Away™ are trademarks of Kari Mecca, and are registered in the United States and abroad. All rights reserved. Whimsy Sticks™ tools and the related methods for creating custom and decorative ornaments are patent pending.

Other fine KP Craft books are available from your favorite bookstore, fabric or craft store or online supplier.

18 17 16 15 14   5 4 3 2 1

DISTRIBUTED IN CANADA BY FRASER DIRECT
100 Armstrong Avenue
Georgetown, ON, Canada L7G 5S4
Tel: (905) 877-4411

DISTRIBUTED IN THE U.K. AND EUROPE
by F&W Media International
LTD Brunel House, Forde Close, Newton Abbot, TQ12 4PU, UK
Tel: (+44) 1626 323200, Fax: (+44) 1626 323319
E-mail: enquiries@fwmedia.com

DISTRIBUTED IN AUSTRALIA BY CAPRICORN LINK
P.O. Box 704, S. Windsor NSW, 2756 Australia
Tel: (02) 4560-11600   Fax: (02) 4577-5288
E-mail: books@capricornlink.com.au

www.fwmedia.com

Edited by *Noel Rivera*

Designed by *Julie Barnett*

Photography by *Braedon Flynn*
of Braedon Photography

Production coordinated by *Greg Nock*

METRIC CONVERSION CHART

TO CONVERT	TO	MULTIPLY BY
inches	centimeters	2.54
centimeters	inches	0.4
feet	centimeters	30.5
centimeters	feet	0.03
yards	meters	0.9
meters	yards	1.1

dedication

To the women in my life…

My daughter, Lauren, who knows just what to say at exactly the right moment. You are beautiful from the inside out.

My friend and office manager, Laurel, whose caring encouragement makes me realize how lucky I am to know her and how very fortunate my customers are.

My friend, Marian, who is outrageously smart, quietly funny and one of the best people I know. Your friendship means more than I can say.

My students and customers, whose curiosity and creativity inspires the same in me. Thank you for your unending support and generosity.

To the men in my life…

My husband, Kris, and my sons, Andrew and Tyler, the amazing men who gracefully accept the things they can't change and love me anyway.

ACKNOWLEDGMENTS

I would first like to thank my friend, Marian Drum, for her ability to understand what I am trying to say and to phrase it perfectly. Thank you to Braedon Flynn for his beautiful photography and kindness over the many photo shoots. To Laurel Himes and my daughter, Lauren Mecca, thank you both for assisting at the photo shoots and for keeping things organized.

I would like to thank everyone at F+W Media who contributed their time and talents to the production of this book. To my editor, Noel Rivera, thank you for your expertise and patience; to designer Julie Barnett, thank you for your creativity and vision; and to Amelia Johansen for getting this project underway and for her talent with words.

To my husband, Kris, thank you for listening when I need to talk things out and for, once again, living with a crazy person. I'm not sure what I would do without you!

About the Author

Kari's eye for the unexpected, combined with her ability to capture the magic of creating, gives her designs a unique appeal to today's seamstress. She is the designer and owner of Kari Me Away, a business catering to those who love embellishing, sewing and hand-embroidery. In addition to this book, she authored *More Sewing with Whimsy*, *Sewing with Whimsy* and *Silk Ribbon Whimsies,* and she coauthored *Silk Ribbon Weaving and Embroidery.* She has developed and manufactures a line of acrylic Whimsy Tools. She also designs and publishes a line of sewing patterns and offers complete kits for her unique designs. As a regular contributor to *Sew Beautiful* magazine, she has seen her designs grace many covers. She is also a regular instructor at Martha Pullen's School of Art Fashion as well as shops and guilds across the country. Her complete product line, including instructional DVDs and the full-sized Whimsy Sticks and Whimsy Tape, can be found at her website www.KariMeAway.com or at a retailer near you.

Inspiration

May these designs inspire you to create beautiful new embellishments!

Make even more fantastic embellishments!

Sewing With Whimsy

by Kari Mecca

Sewing with Whimsy is a fanciful treat in children's sewing and embellishing. Kari Mecca's one-of-a-kind projects and ideas range from fun and funky to sweet and sassy. Techniques include creating magical rickrack flowers and trims, making and applying beautiful ribbon flowers, adding sparkle with beads and heirloom sewing techniques.

ISBN-13: 978-1-8780-4852-3

More Sewing With Whimsy

by Kari Mecca

More Sewing with Whimsy is filled with flirty flounces, waving bias, spaghetti appliqué and Kari's own touch of fairy dust—her newly created collection of Whimsy Sticks. Kari's signature styling is nowhere more evident than in the fanciful embellishments she creates using her Whimsy Sticks. Includes full-sized patterns in girls' sizes 2–8.

ISBN-13: 978-1-8780-4861-5

 Try even more of our great sewing titles at sewdaily.com!

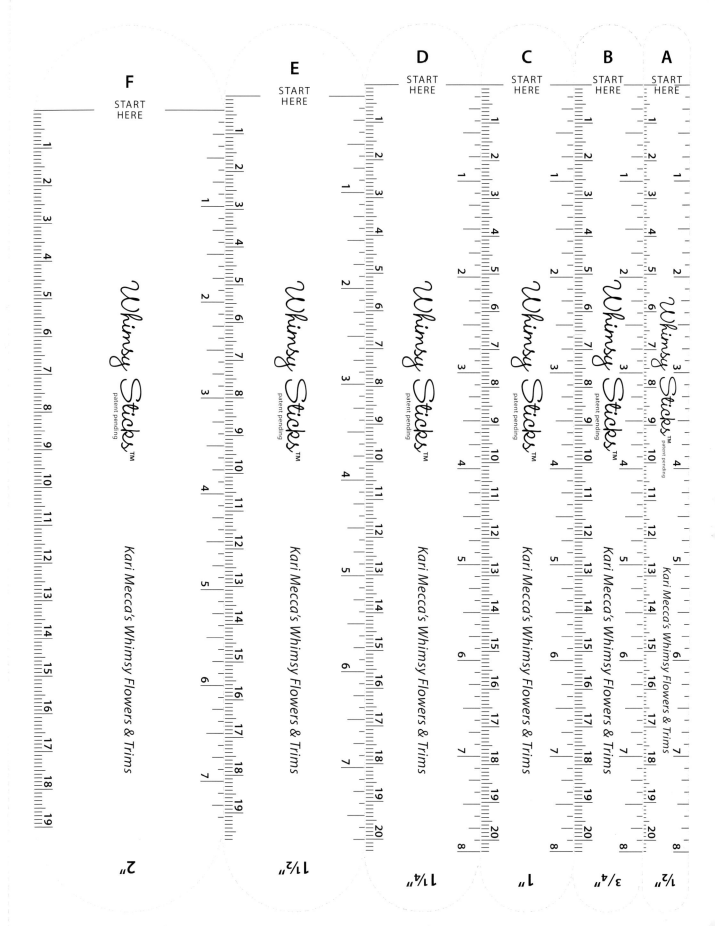